TR897.7 .H68 2006

Hosea, Birgitta.

The Focal easy guide to
  Macromedia Flash 8 : for
    2006.

2008 09 26

MACROMEDIA
FLASH 8

The Focal Easy Guide Series

Focal Easy Guides are the best choice to get you started with new software, whatever your level. Refreshingly simple, they do not attempt to cover everything, focusing solely on the essentials needed to get immediate results.

Ideal if you need to learn a new software package quickly, the Focal Easy Guides offer an effective, time-saving introduction to the key tools, not hundreds of pages of confusing reference material. The emphasis is on quickly getting to grips with the software in a practical and accessible way to achieve professional results.

Highly illustrated in color, explanations are short and to the point. Written by professionals in a user-friendly style, the guides assume some computer knowledge and an understanding of the general concepts in the area covered, ensuring they aren't patronizing!

Series editor: Rick Young (www.digitalproduction.net)

Director and Founding Member of the UK Final Cut User Group, Apple Solutions Expert and freelance television director/editor, Rick has worked for the BBC, Sky, ITN, CNBC and Reuters. Also a Final Cut Pro Consultant and author of the best-selling *The Easy Guide to Final Cut Pro*.

Titles in the series:

The Focal Easy Guide to After Effects, **Curtis Sponsler**
The Focal Easy Guide to Cakewalk Sonar, **Trev Wilkins**
The Focal Easy Guide to DVD Studio Pro 3, **Rick Young**
The Focal Easy Guide to Final Cut Express, **Rick Young**
The Easy Guide to Final Cut Pro 3, **Rick Young**
The Focal Easy Guide to Final Cut Pro 4, **Rick Young**
The Focal Easy Guide to Final Cut Pro 5, **Rick Young**
The Focal Easy Guide to Discreet combustion 3, **Gary M. Davis**
The Focal Easy Guide to Combustion 4, **Gary M. Davis**
The Focal Easy Guide to Maya 5, **Jason Patnode**
The Focal Easy Guide to Premiere Pro, **Tim Kolb**
The Focal Easy Guide to Flash MX 2004, **Birgitta Hosea**

THE FOCAL EASY GUIDE TO
MACROMEDIA FLASH 8

/6020/

For new users and professionals

BIRGITTA HOSEA

AMSTERDAM • BOSTON • HEIDELBERG • LONDON • NEW YORK • OXFORD
PARIS • SAN DIEGO • SAN FRANCISCO • SINGAPORE • SYDNEY • TOKYO
Focal Press is an imprint of Elsevier

ELSEVIER

Focal
Press

Focal Press is an imprint of Elsevier
Linacre House, Jordan Hill, Oxford OX2 8DP, UK
30 Corporate Drive, Suite 400, Burlington, MA 01803, USA

First edition 2006
Reprinted 2007

Notice
No responsibility is assumed by the publisher for any injury and/or damage to persons
or property as a matter of products liability, negligence or otherwise, or from any use
or operation of any methods, products, instructions or ideas contained in the material
herein. Because of rapid advances in the medical sciences, in particular, independent
verification of diagnoses and drug dosages should be made

British Library Cataloguing in Publication Data
A catalogue record for this book is available from the British Library

Library of Congress Cataloging-in-Publication Data
A catalog record for this book is available from the Library of Congress

ISBN: 978-0-240-51998-2

For information on all Focal Press publications
visit our website at www.focalpress.com

Printed and bound in China

07 08 09 10   10 9 8 7 6 5 4 3 2

Working together to grow
libraries in developing countries

www.elsevier.com | www.bookaid.org | www.sabre.org

ELSEVIER   BOOK AID
International   Sabre Foundation

Contents

4   Selecting and Modifying

5   Importing Images

CHAPTER 1
INTRODUCTION

History and Development of the Program

SmartSketch was a drawing application originally developed in the early 1990s by Jonathan Gay and his company Future Splash, which developed into an animation program for the Internet – FutureSplash Animator. Future Splash was a small company with one of many multimedia plug-ins struggling for attention. It was offered for sale to Adobe who initially turned it down due to its unimpressive performance!

Although the early versions were slow and buggy, Disney started using it along with Shockwave and this attracted the attention of Macromedia. The Shockwave Flash plug-in format was then developed by Macromedia to play back small and fast vector animated content on the web. In December 1996 Flash 1 was born.

Flash is now in version 8. It has evolved into a sophisticated package for the creation of economical animation and interactive content. Due to its popularity, many other drawing and animation programs now have a Shockwave Flash export option.

To read more about the history of Flash, go to **<http://www.macromedia.com/macromedia/events/john_gay>**.

The New and Exciting Flash 2 from 1997

What Is It Used for?

Flash is used for the creation of graphics, animation and media that users can interact with, such as interfaces, rich media web pages, games, real-time chat applications, interactive shopping systems and video conferencing. Although the program is primarily associated with creating content for the Internet, Flash is also used to create stand-alone CD-ROMS and presentations, animation for TV, content for PDAs, interactive television, kiosks and mobile phones.

How to Use This Book

The potential of this program is vast and it would be impossible to cover every single feature in one little Easy Guide. Since the launch of Flash MX 2004, there are now two versions of the program – standard and professional. This book can be used with both versions.

The **Easy Guide to Flash** is designed to introduce you to the fundamentals of Flash – creating vector graphics, animation and basic interactivity, incorporating video and sound, and exporting from the program to the Internet and to video.

File	Edit	Commands
New...		⌘N
Open...		⌘O
Open from Site...		
Open Recent		▶
Close		⌘W
Close All		
Save		⌘S
Save and Compact		
Save As...		⇧⌘S
Save as Template...		
Save All		
Import		▶
Page Setup...		
Print Margins...		
Print...		⌘P
Edit Sites...		

File > New

When you have finished this book, if you are interested in learning more about ActionScripting or outputting to any of the more specialized delivery platforms there is a list of further resources on the accompanying website – www.easyguidetoflash.com

Each chapter covers one aspect of the program and contains step-by-step tutorials to enable you to start straight away. This book is extensively illustrated with screen shots from the program. The screen shot illustrations have been created on both Mac and PC as the author works on both, and is platform-agnostic. Shortcuts for both platforms have been given.

This book uses certain conventions in order to avoid repetition and save space. In the case of choosing options from the various menus, the

3

abbreviation **File** > **New** is used instead of saying go to the **File** menu then choose the **New** command from the dropdown list of options.

Both Mac and PC shortcuts are given throughout. Instead of writing them both out in full, the following conventions are used:

- For the **Command** key (Mac) ⌘ is used, followed by **CTRL** for the **Control** key, which is the PC equivalent. For example, the keyboard shortcut for **File** > **New** is written as ⌘/CTRL + N.

- **ALT** is used throughout as an abbreviation for the **Option** key (Mac) and **ALT** key (PC).

- PC users have a right mouse button, which can be used to open context sensitive menus when you apply it to different parts of the program. The Mac equivalent of a right mouse click is to hold down the **CTRL** key. This is abbreviated throughout as **CTRL/RIGHT-CLICK**.

- Another convention used throughout the book is that the final product of your Flash project is referred to as a '**movie**'. Of course your end product need not be animation. It could be a web site or even a CD-ROM, but to simplify matters it is referred to as a '**movie**'.

There is a supporting web site to go with this book at **<www.easyguidetoflash.com>** where you can download examples used in this book. You can also post your own tips and tricks for other readers to see as well as links to flash web sites that you have created.

Finally, you will only ever really start to learn a piece of software when you apply it to your own projects. This book is designed to provide you with a fundamental vocabulary in Flash. The rest is up to you. Use the exercises here as a starting point, adapt and change them to suit your own designs and ideas, and you will be fluent in Flash in no time!

CHAPTER 2
INTERFACE

Flash 8 has interface elements that are common to all Macromedia web and multimedia authoring products. So, once you are familiar with one of the Macromedia programs, you will be on your way to understanding the others.

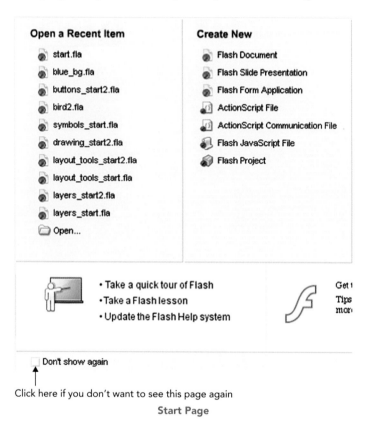

Click here if you don't want to see this page again

Start Page

The Start Page

1 The Start Page allows you to quickly access files and create new items. When you first begin to use the program it is worthwhile spending some time taking the quick tour of Flash and taking some of the in-built Flash lessons, which you can access from this page.

2 If you don't want to see this page again, click in the check box to select **Don't show again**. If you want to make sure that this page will open each time you open Flash, you need to select this in the preferences. To do this on a Mac, go to **Flash** > **Preferences** > **On launch** > **Show Start Page**.

Preferences. Circle Indicates 'Show Start Page'

3   To do this on a PC, go to **Edit** > **Preferences** > **On Launch** > **Show Start Page**.

At a Glance Guide to the Interface

The Interface at a Glance

Menus – Just as in any other software program, access different parts of the software by choosing from the menus at the top of the screen.

Stage – This is where you create and view your design work.

Workspace – The gray area off the edge of the Stage that won't be seen in the final movie. It can be shown or hidden by choosing **View > Work Area**. The size of this area has been expanded in Flash 8.

Tools – Select a tool to create, select, refine and manipulate design elements. See Chapters 3 and 4 for details about using these tools.

Timeline – A grid showing each frame of the Flash movie. It enables you to work with the element of time moving horizontally from left to right. The numbers along the top refer to the number of frames in your movie.

Edit Bar – Shows which scene or symbol you are working on and allows you to change the magnification of the view on the right. Can be turned on or off by selecting **Window > Toolbars > Edit Bar**.

Layers – Elements can be separated into layers to keep them distinct. This is essential if you want to animate them. Layers are stacked vertically – one on top of each other like sheets of paper. See Chapter 6 for more information about layers.

Panel Sets – Additional windows allowing you to control and manipulate your design elements as well as adding interactivity. These are accessed through the **Windows** menu.

Properties Inspector – This is context sensitive and changes according to which part of the interface is selected. To see this in action, click on different tools, one after the other, and see how it changes.

If it is not visible, select **Window > Properties**.

What are all the Windows for?

The Stage

1   The Stage is like your drawing board – it's where all the action happens. The size of the Stage defines the size of your final Flash movie. You can

change the size of your movie by selecting **Modify > Document**. This launches the **Document Properties**.

Size Button

Size Button

2 You can also open this window by first clicking on the background of your Stage to select it and then by clicking on the **size** button in the **Properties Inspector**.

Document Properties

Title: name of your project

Description: add metadata here, i.e. key words and phrases that you would like WWW Search Engines to associate with this page

Dimensions: 768 px (width) x 576 px (height)

Match: ◯ Printer   ◯ Contents   ◯ Default

Background color:

Frame rate: 25 fps

Ruler units: Pixels

Make Default   OK   Cancel

Document Properties

3 The Document Properties window controls the pixel dimensions of the Stage and, therefore, of the final movie. These dimensions are 550 × 400 pixels by default. The smallest size you can have is 1 × 1 pixels and the largest is 2880 × 2880 pixels.

4   Chapter 13 discusses several possible sizes for banner ads and whole web sites. It is good practice to set the size of your Stage right at the beginning of working on your document. If you resize the Stage towards the end of working on your document, you may have to re-position all your elements and this could be time consuming.

Background Color

5   The background color of your document can be changed by clicking, holding and then sliding the mouse down from the **background color swatch** to select whichever color you choose.

6   The ruler units can be changed to measure in inches, points, centimeters and milli- meters as well as pixels. It is advisable to keep this as **pixels** unless you are using Flash to create illus-

Ruler Units

trations for print. Screen based work such as web sites and animation for video are measured in pixels.

7   If there is a size, background color and frame rate that you usually use – click on the **default** button so that you will automatically use these settings in all new files you create.

Make Default

The Timeline

The Timeline

1 The Timeline allows you to create and edit animations – to move forwards and backwards in time.

Measured in Frames

2 The units of measurement along the top of the ruler are in frames.

A keyframe

One Frame Movie

3 The length of your movie is controlled by how many keyframes and frames you have created in the Timeline. In this example there is only one keyframe. This means that this movie doesn't have any time to move – it is actually a still image.

Drag the playhead to see what is happening on different frames

Frames Keyframe

This number shows the number of the frame that the playhead is on

Reminder of the frame rate measured in frames per second. This is set in the document properties and double clicking on this number is a short cut to open that window

A 25-frame Movie

4   In this example there are 25 frames and the frame rate is set at 25 frames per second, so there is one second of animation. For more information about keyframes see Chapter 6. There is more about frame rate in Chapter 8.

Changing Your View

1   The **Zoom** tool allows you to magnify your view. ⌘/**CTRL** + − **or** + also allows you to do this. Double-clicking on the **Zoom** tool icon in the **Toolbox** resets your view to 100%.

View

The Hand Tool   The Zoom Tool

The View Tools

2   Pressing and holding down the spacebar allows you to toggle to the **Hand** tool even though you are on the **Zoom** tool.

3   The **Hand** tool allows you to move around the area that you are viewing. Double-clicking on the **Hand** tool centers your frame within the work area.

4   The scale of your view can also be chosen in the **Stage magnification** options in the **Edit Bar** at the top of your **Timeline**. If you can't see it choose **Window** > **Toolbars** > **Edit Bar**.

The Stage Magnification Options in the Edit Bar

Panel Sets and Customizing Your Interface

1 There are many extra small windows called **Panels**, which add extra
functionality to Flash and can be opened through the **Window** menu.
These will be covered in more detail in the chapter that covers their
individual functions.

2 If all of the Panels were open at once you would need a really large
monitor to see them all! This is not necessary, however, because you
can customize your interface to suit the way in which you are working.

3 The easiest way to customize your interface is to press **F4** to hide or
open Tools, Panels and Properties.

Color Mixer Panel Collapsed

▼ Color

Color Mixer Panel Expanded

4 The **Timeline** and the **Panels** can all be collapsed. This is done by clicking
on the little triangle to the left of the window's name.

Panel Options Menu (Circled)

5 You don't have to have the default Panels open that were there when you first installed Flash. You can choose which Panels you want to have open. To close a Panel, click on the

Close Panel (Circled)

Options menu on the right hand side of its title and choose **Close Panel**.

6 The Panels are all dockable. This means you can group them with other Panels or change their position. If you move your mouse so that the cursor is over the **Panel handle**, the icon will change. You can now drag a Panel out of a docked position.

Panel Handle (Circled)

7 If you want to add a Panel to a group of Panels so that it will become docked, drag the Panel over the position that you want it to have in the Panel group. You will see a dark line overlapping the position this Panel will take.

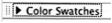

Panel Overlap

Let go and the Panel will be in its new position.

8 There are some clever keyboard shortcuts that you can use with Panels. If you select ⌘/**CTRL** +

Color Swatches

Panel Focus

ALT + TAB this puts a **'focus'** on the Timeline or uppermost Panel. You can then press this key combination again to cycle through Panels.

9   Once you have a Panel in 'focus', then the **Up** and **Down** arrow keys also cycle through the Panels and the **Space Bar** collapses/expands the Panel in 'focus'.

10 When you have selected the Panels you want to use and moved them into your preferred position, you can save the Panel layout. In fact, you could save different layouts for working in different areas of the program, e.g. drawing, animating, creating buttons etc.

Save Workspace Layout

Name: my favorite

OK   Cancel

Save Panel Layout

11 To do this, go to **Window > Workspace Layout > Save Current**, name your Panel arrangement and click **OK**. This arrangement will now be available for you in **Window > Workspace Layout**.

12 The Panels that I find most useful from a Designer's perspective to save into a Panel set are the following: **Color Mixer**, **Color Swatches**, **Transform**, **Align**, and the **Library**.

Using the Help files

1   The Help files contain lots of detailed explanation about all areas of Flash. The Help menu allows you to jump to different parts of the Help files. In the **Help > Getting Started with Flash** section, you can access lessons on all the basic features of the program.

2   **Help > Flash Help** takes you straight to sections of information covering all of the different areas.

Flash Documents

1   When you work in Flash, the type of file that you are working on is a **Flash document** or **FLA** file. If you want to change or do more work on

your Flash document or to open it on another computer – **select File > Save** and save the FLA file. Give it a name related to the contents so that you can remember what it contained.

2   From this Flash document, you can export other files that can then be put onto a web page or burnt onto a DVD. This will be covered in more detail in Chapters 14 and 15.

Naming Files and Working Cross-platform

1   PC file names generally have a three-letter extension at the end. The extension for a **FLA** file is **.fla**, e.g. **mydocument.fla.** What these three letters do is instruct the PC as to the type of file that it is referring to.

2   A Macintosh computer doesn't work in the same way and doesn't need the **.fla** filename extension to enable it to recognize the file type.

3   So, if you want to work cross-platform, you have to think about file naming conventions. If you create a Flash document on a Macintosh and have named it with a PC style three letter extension, e.g. **mydocument.fla**, then it should open on a PC without a problem.

File name:	start.fla	∨	Save
Save as type:	Flash MX 2004 Document (*.fla)	∨	Cancel
	Flash 8 Document (*.fla)		
	Flash MX 2004 Document (*.fla)		

Saving as a Flash MX Document

4   Even though you may be working with the latest version of Flash – Flash 8 – you may find yourself working with people who have the previous version of the program. If you save as a Flash 8 file, you will only be able to open it on Flash 8. However, you can choose **File > Save As Type > Flash MX 2004 Document.** This file can then be opened on Flash MX 2004, although certain new MX new Flash 8 features such as behaviors will not be preserved.

5   Finally, don't forget to save your work regularly. Occasionally any program can crash while you are working and if you have saved recently this will only be a minor inconvenience.

What is vector drawing? It is a way to create and save digital imaging information. The edges are crisp, the colors are flat and the artwork you create is editable. In other words, you can go back to a graphic that you have created and easily modify its outline, color, etc. Getting to know the drawing Tools and all the different mark making possibilities in the program, is the first step towards developing your own original style in Flash.

At a Glance Guide to the Tools

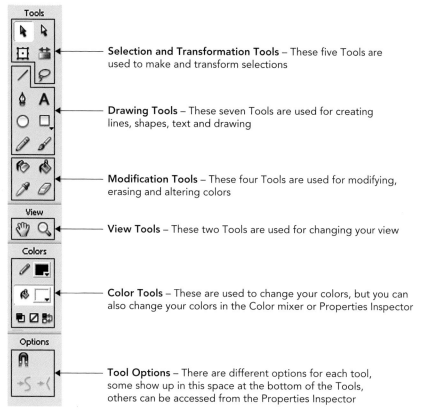

Selection and Transformation Tools – These five Tools are used to make and transform selections

Drawing Tools – These seven Tools are used for creating lines, shapes, text and drawing

Modification Tools – These four Tools are used for modifying, erasing and altering colors

View Tools – These two Tools are used for changing your view

Color Tools – These are used to change your colors, but you can also change your colors in the Color mixer or Properties Inspector

Tool Options – There are different options for each tool, some show up in this space at the bottom of the Tools, others can be accessed from the Properties Inspector

The Tools

The Drawing Tools

When you create a piece of artwork in Flash, it is known as a '**shape**'. The outline is called the '**stroke**' and the center is called the '**fill**'.

Fill   Stroke   A Shape

Colors

Click and hold to change the Fill/Stroke Color

Fill and Stroke Colors

Drawing a Line

1   You can create many different types of lines in Flash. After selecting the **Line** tool, you then choose the **stroke** attributes in the **Toolbox**, **Properties Inspector** or in the **Color panel**.

The Line Tool

2   Click and drag the line on the Stage. Click a second time to end the line.

3   Holding down shift while you are dragging a line, constrains it to increments of 45°.

4   When the **Line** tool is being used, you are able to access options for your line in the **Properties Inspector** as shown in the diagram above. Clicking on the **Custom** button opens the **Stroke Style** window, which gives you lots of different options to create lines with different textures.

Line Thickness   Select a Line Style   Customize Your   Change the Shape of
Line Style   the End of Your Line

To Change Line Color

Prevents Blurry Lines

Choose a Shape for
the Corner of a Path

Allows You to Constrain
the Rescaling of the Line

The Line Tool Properties Inspector

Stroke Styles

5   Explore and experiment with all the different line styles to create
texture and diversity in your drawing. As of Flash 8, strokes can go up
to a thickness of 200 pixels.

6   NB. If you are creating
animation that you later
want to put onto video,
avoid the hairline
thickness option.
When used on video
one pixel thin lines can
seem to jitter. More on
this in Chapter 12.

Line Options

7 The ability to be able to change the ends of lines (or **Caps**) and to be able to choose **Corner** styles is new to Flash 8.

Round

None

Square

Caps

8 Because these are new features, your project needs to be compatible with Flash Player Version 8 in order for them to be supported. To make sure that the file you are working on is compatible with Flash Player 8, select **File** > **Publish Settings** > **Flash** > **Version** > **Flash Player 8**.

Publish Settings

Current profile: Default

| Formats | Flash | HTML |

Version: Flash Player 8

Setting the Publish Settings to Flash Player 8

9 The corner settings work on a Path and not a straightforward line drawn with the Line tool.

Drawing with the Pencil Tool

1 The **Pencil** tool is another way to create lines, that is, **strokes**. So, as with the **Line** tool, when the **Pencil** tool is selected, you can choose a color from the **Stroke Color Control** in the Toolbox or the Color Mixer panel.

The Pencil Tool

2 You can also select the stroke color as well as customizing the style of the stroke in the Properties Inspector just as with the **Line** tool.

3 In addition, if you draw a corner with the **Pencil** tool, you will be able to choose the style of the join.

Round   Miter   Bevel   **Corner Styles**

4 In the **Options** section at the bottom of the **Toolbox**, you can choose a drawing mode. The drawing modifiers selected effect how Flash processes the lines you draw. **Straighten** will straighten out your lines and recognize simple shapes, **Smooth** will give more smooth curves and **Ink** allows you to draw free hand, leaving the line exactly as you drew it without modification.

Pencil Tool Drawing Modifiers

A Similar Shape Drawn in Pencil with Each of the Different Modifiers Selected

The Shape Tools

1 The **Oval**, **Rectangle** and **PolyStar** Tools are used in a similar way to the **Line** tool. The **PolyStar** tool is accessed by clicking and holding on the **Rectangle** tool.

Shape Tools

2 The **stroke color and style** can be selected and the stroke style customized in the Properties Inspector, just as with the **Line** and **Pencil** tools. The **fill color** can also be chosen here.

3 Holding down **SHIFT** while you are drawing an oval or a rectangle constrains the proportions so that you end up with a perfect circle or square.

4 The **PolyStar** tool has an extra set of style options in the Properties Inspector. These are reached by clicking on **Options** and allow you to choose polygon or star, the number of sides and the depth of the points on a star.

Tool Settings

Style	star
Number of Sides	12
Star point size	0.50

Cancel   OK

PolyStar Tool Settings

5 The **Rectangle** tool has Options available at the bottom of the Toolbox. If **Snap to Objects** is selected, you will feel a slight magnetic pull when your rectangle is near other shapes.

Options

Snap to Objects   Rounded Corners

Rectangle Tool Options

6 When you select the **rounded corner** option, the Rectangle Settings window opens. This prompts you to add a figure, which defines how curved the corner will be.

Rectangle Settings

Corner radius: 15 points   OK

Cancel

Rectangle Rounded Corner Settings

7 If you prefer to set the roundness of your corners visually, use the **Up** and **Down** arrow keys while you are drawing your rectangle – don't take your finger off your mouse.

8 If you have either the **Oval** or **Rectangle** tool selected in the **Toolbox**, hold down the **ALT** key and then click on the **Stage**, you will open up the Oval or Rectangle Settings box.

Oval Settings

Width: 100 pixels   OK

Height: 100 pixels   Cancel

☑ Draw from center

Oval Settings

Painting with the Brush Tool

1 You can change the color of the **Brush** tool in the
Toolbox, **Properties Inspector** or the **Color Mixer**
panel, however unlike the **Line** and the **Pencil** Tools the
color of this tool is changed in the **fill** color control.

The Brush Tool

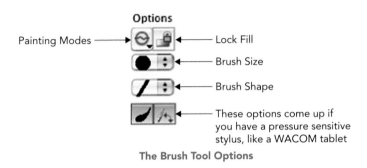

The Brush Tool Options

2 From these Options, you can choose your brush size and shape. As the
Brush tool is painting with fills and not a stroke, you can't change the
line style.

3 Holding down the **SHIFT** key while you paint constrains the **Brush** to go
in a horizontal or vertical direction only.

The Painting Modes

4 Tablets, like the WACOM Intuos pictured, connect to a USB port
and can be used at the same time as your mouse or as a replacement.

If you use a tablet and pen to draw with instead of a mouse, you will have options to apply pressure and sensitivity to the line you create – just like with a real pencil. If you do a lot of digital artwork, this can be a good way to avoid repetitive strain injury in your wrist.

The WACOM Intuos 3 Pen and Tablet

The Brush Tool Allows You to Create Gestural Marks and Get Away from a Flat 'Computery' Look. Using the Brush Tool Along with a WACOM Tablet Gives You More Control Over Your Drawing

Using the Pen Tool and the Subselection Tool

1   The **Pen** tool is used to create anchor points with connecting lines – just like a game of 'join the dots'! First select your required **fill** and **stroke** colors and then click to make angular, corner points – each click of the mouse creates another anchor point.

The Pen Tool

2 Holding down **SHIFT** when you click restricts the angles of the lines you are creating to multiples of 45°.

3 Clicking and dragging makes a curved, bezier point. Double-clicking on the last point ends the shape. When the path that the anchor points make is joined up, the shape will fill with color. You can also close the path by clicking on the first point that you made.

Drag on the handles to alter the curve

Bezier Curves with the Pen Tool

4 Drag on the handles to alter the curvature of the line. Holding down the **ALT** key when you drag on a handle allows you to move it independently from its partner.

ALT + drag on the handles to move them independently

Bezier Curves with the Pen Tool

5 As you move the **Pen** tool, the cursor changes if you are near a point or the line created. You can delete, modify or add points according to where the **Pen** tool is.

| To create an entirely new point | To add a point on a section of line | To delete a point | To close a path and end a shape |

To convert a curve point to a corner point. After you have clicked on this option, a second click will take you to the delete point option

Pen Tool Icons

6   Using the **Subselection** tool allows you to convert a shape you have drawn with any of the drawing Tools into anchor points. These points can then be carefully selected and moved individually – using the **arrow** keys nudges these points one pixel at a time. Using **SHIFT** + **arrow** keys moves the points further. You can also delete them with the **delete** key on your keyboard.

The Subselection Tool

7   The **Pen** tool can be used to add, delete or convert anchor points on shapes that you have drawn with other Tools.

8   A corner point can also be turned into a curved path by selecting the point with the **Subselection** tool, holding down the **ALT** key and dragging out a curve. If you want to try the opposite and turn a curved point into a corner point, hold down the **ALT** key and double-click to convert it.

An anchor point is darker when it is selected. By default, a curved point appears as a dark circle when it is selected and a corner point appears as a square

9   NB. Sometimes when you use the **Subselection** tool to adjust a shape, extra new points will be added by the software.

To Overlap or to Obliterate: Object Drawing vs. Merge Drawing

There are two different ways of creating shapes in Flash: **Object Drawing** or **Merge Drawing**. The difference between them is what happens when two shapes overlap. This is a new feature of Flash 8.

The mode that is selected by default when you first start using Flash 8 is **Merge Drawing**. This means that if you overlap one shape with another of the same color, after it is de-selected it will become joined to the first shape.

Before, Drawing a shape on top and After this new shape is removed

Cutting a Hole

If the second shape is not the same color as the first, it will cut a hole in the first shape underneath. You can use this effect deliberately to create holes in shapes, but you may wish to avoid this happening all together.

**Merge Drawing Selected
in the Toolbox Options**

**Object Drawing Selected
in the Toolbox Options**

All of the **drawing tools** have an **Object Drawing** option down in the **Tools Options** section of the **Toolbox**.

If you select this option, each element remains separate and will have a blue bounding line around it. You can now overlap shapes without altering what is underneath.

Changing Colors

1 We have already seen how colors can be selected in the **Toolbox** and the **Properties Inspector**. If you want to create a shape without an outline, select the **Stroke Color Control** and then choose **no color**.

The Color Tools

2 The **Color Swatches** panel is another convenient way to select colors. If you can't see this panel, choose **Window** > **Color Swatches** to open it.

The Color Mixer and Color Swatches Panels

3   There are several ways to create new colors in the **Color Mixer** panel. If you can't see this panel, choose **Window** > **Color Mixer** to open it.

4   If you are creating a web site and know the precise color that you want to use, you can type in the **hexadecimal code**. This is a system of using letters and numbers to describe a color for use on the web.

5   You can also move the **red, green, blue** and **alpha** (transparency) **sliders** to subtly change a color's component parts.

6   Finally, you can also click around in the **color space** to define a color and then drag the **brightness** slider to alter its tonality.

Creating Gradient Fills

1   Choose **Linear** or **Radial** from the **Fill Type** pop-up menu in **Color Mixer** panel.

Creating a Gradient Fill

2 As of Flash 8, you can create complex gradients containing up to 16 colors by adding more pointers. To change the colors in your gradient, click on a **pointer** to select it, then change its color by dragging in the **Color Space**. Double-clicking on a pointer opens up **Color Swatches** that you can select.

Color Mixer Options Menu

3 When you have created a gradient fill, you can save it for re-use. Click on the **Color Mixer** Options menu and choose **Add Swatch**.

Swatch Added

4 Your gradient fill is now available for you at the bottom of the **Color Swatches**.

5 Another new feature of Flash 8 is that gradients can now be applied to strokes as well as fills.

Transform Fill Tool

6 Your gradient fill can be altered, re-sized and re-angled after you have created it with the **Transform Fill** tool. Select this tool in the Toolbox and then click on the shape whose gradient you want to alter.

Transform Fill Tool

Default fill. The gradient is symmetrical and centered on the shape

Click and drag to re-position

Squash or stretch

Rotate

Re-scale proportionally

Using the Transform Fill Tool

7 If you want your **gradient fill** to extend across several shapes on the Stage, select the **Lock Fill** modifier in the **Toolbox** from the **Brush** or **Paint Bucket** tool. Now each shape you fill with the **Paint Bucket** or paint with the **Brush** tool will share the same gradient.

Shapes with Lock Fill Applied so that One Gradient is Spread Across All of the Shapes

Creating Text

1 Text is created in Flash with the **Text** tool and the style
of the text is changed in the **Properties Inspector.**

The Text Tool

Text orientation –
vertical or horizontal

Leave on Static text.
The other options are
for dynamically updated
text and form fields

Click here to
see the pop-up
list of fonts

Font size

Paragraph format
spacing options

Bold or italic

Font color

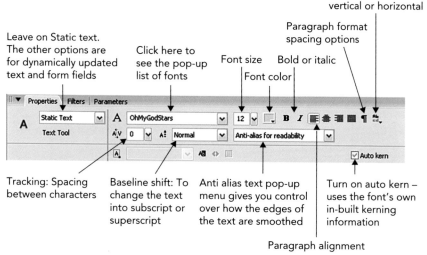

Tracking: Spacing
between characters

Baseline shift: To
change the text
into subscript or
superscript

Anti alias text pop-up
menu gives you control
over how the edges of
the text are smoothed

Turn on auto kern –
uses the font's own
in-built kerning
information

Paragraph alignment

The Text Tool Properties

2 After you have selected the **Text** tool, you can either click on the Stage
to type letters all in a line or you can click and drag out a type box. This
will allow you to type continuously into a box with a fixed width.

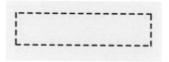

An Empty Type Box

3 As well as typing into Flash,
when you use the Text tool you
can copy and paste text
information from another
text program on your computer.

Typing with a Fixed Width

4 Text in Flash is editable, this means that when your text is selected you can alter properties like font, size and color as well as re-typing the letters.

Selected Text

5 When on the **Text** tool, you can click and drag over the text to highlight part of it. This will allow you to use different styles on different parts of your text.

Different Text Styles

6 When your text is highlighted and you click on the pop-menu to change the font, you will see a preview of your chosen text in all the different fonts as you scroll up and down them.

EASY GUIDE

Text that has been Broken Apart into Graphic Shapes and Then the Shape of the Letters have been Altered by Using the *Subselection* Tool

Text that has been Broken Apart into Individual Letters

7 To convert your editable text into a shape, select the text, then **Modify** > **Break Apart**. This breaks the text into individual letters. Apply **Modify** > **Break Apart** a second time and the letters will be understood by Flash as a graphic shape and not as editable text.

8 The result is that these letters will now look the same on any computer – no matter which fonts the system has loaded. The down side is that this process can add to the file size and may be frustrating if you want to go back and alter the wording of the text.

9 The Anti alias pop-up menu gives you some other options.

Use device fonts – The options are _sans, _serif or_typewriter. A generic related font on the users computer will then be selected. Device fonts are especially clear and can be good to use if you want to include small letters at 8 points or less

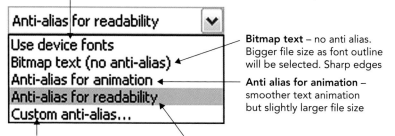

Bitmap text – no anti alias. Bigger file size as font outline will be selected. Sharp edges

Anti alias for animation – smoother text animation but slightly larger file size

In order to use the **custom** option you must publish to Flash Player 8

Anti alias for readability – good for small sizes but will only work if file is published for Flash Player 8

Anti Alias Pop-Up Menu

Paragraph Options

These are similar to the standard options in a typical word processing program.

To set right/left margins click here or add a number

To specify line spacing

To specify indents

Paragraph Options

Spell Checker

1 Go to **Text** > **Check Spelling** to check the spelling in your document. You have the choice to **ignore** the spelling advice given or **change**.

2 If you commonly use certain words that the program considers you are spelling 'wrong', then select **Add to Personal** to remember this in future.

3 **Text** > **Spelling Set** Up allows you to personalize the spelling options.

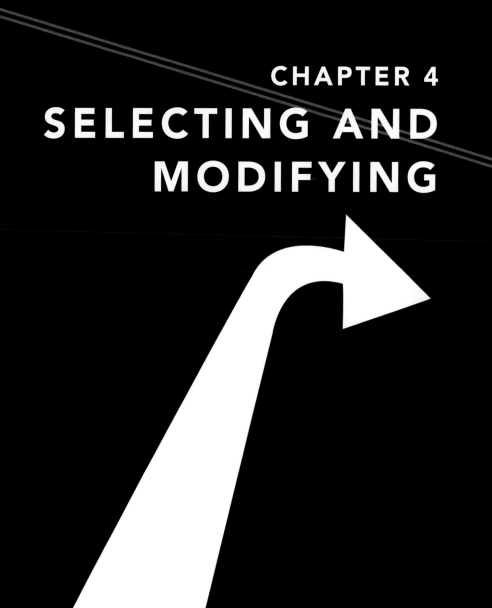

CHAPTER 4
SELECTING AND
MODIFYING

As we have seen in the previous chapter, the beauty of vector drawing is that it is so easily adaptable. Basic artwork is known as shape data and can be edited, molded and manipulated.

Making Selections

1 If you have created a shape with a **fill** and a **stroke**, clicking it once with the **Selection** tool will only select the **fill**. To select all drawn elements connected to one shape, double click with the **Selection** tool.

The Selection Tool

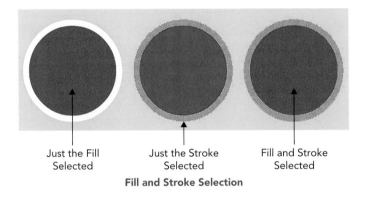

Just the Fill   Just the Stroke   Fill and Stroke
Selected   Selected   Selected

Fill and Stroke Selection

2 To select several shapes within a rectangular marquee area, click and drag a box around all the shapes with the **Selection** tool. Symbols, groups and text objects must be completely enclosed to be selected.

3 You can also duplicate with the **Selection** tool. **SHIFT + drag** selection makes a copy.

4 To create an area of selection by drawing, use the **Lasso** tool. When the cursor is over a selected element, the **Lasso** tool becomes an arrow that you can use to move the element.

The Lasso Tool

5 To make multiple marquee or **Lasso** tool selections, press **SHIFT** while you lasso or marquee-select.

6 To select everything on every layer of the scene, choose **Edit** > **Select All**, or press ⌘/**CTRL** + **A**.

7 To deselect everything on every layer, choose **Edit** > **Deselect All**, or press ⌘/**CTRL** + **SHIFT** + **A**.

Modifying Drawings

1 The **Selection** tool can also be used to modify drawings. When you have this tool selected in the toolbox and move your cursor around a shape you have created that is not selected, the icon will change according to whether it is over a line, a corner or away from a shape.

Selection Cursor Over a Line   Over a Corner

2 If you are over a line and see the first icon, you can drag on the line and pull out a curve.

3 If you are over a corner and see the second icon, you can pull out the corner.

4 If you are over a line and hold down the **ALT** key, you can pull a corner point out of a line.

5 This is a good method to quickly sculpt shapes into the form you require. In the last chapter, we saw how the **Subselection** tool used in conjunction with the **Pen** tool gives very precise control over your drawing. Sometimes, however, it is better to work quicker and rougher, and create your basic shape before refining it further, rather than being very careful and drawing a complex shape from the beginning.

6 If you select a shape with the **Selection** tool and then click on the **Straighten** option – the outline of the shape will become straighter and more angular. Clicking on the **Smoothing** option will make your shape have smoother curves.

Options

Snap to Objects

Smooth

Straighten

The Selection Tool Options

7 This can also be done through the **Modify** menu by choosing **Modify > Smooth** or **Modify > Shape > Straighten**.

8 Turning on **Snap to Objects** will give you a slight magnetic pull when one shape is near another.

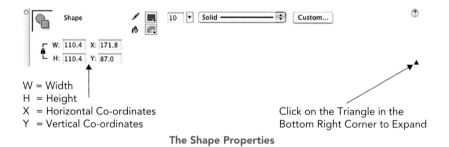

W = Width
H = Height
X = Horizontal Co-ordinates
Y = Vertical Co-ordinates

Click on the Triangle in the Bottom Right Corner to Expand

The Shape Properties

9 When you have selected a shape with the **Selection** tool, you can see the properties of the **Shape** in the **Properties Inspector**. Expanding this window allows you to see the W, H, X and Y figures. By entering x and y co-ordinates in Properties Inspector, the shape can be moved in exact amounts.

10 There are several other ways to alter shapes you have drawn through the **Modify > Shape** menu. **Convert Line to Fill** – this changes any lines you have selected into a filled shape. **Shape** > **Expand Fill** – this allows you to expand or reduce a filled shape. **Shape** > **Soften Fill Edges** – this can give your shapes a softer edge, but increases the file size.

The Free Transform Tool

1 When you select this tool, you can rotate the selection by moving the cursor just outside the corner handles or move the selection by dragging from a central position. The white dot is the center point. Dragging this to a new position will change your center of transformation. It will not change the position of your shape.
Drag out the corners to rescale.

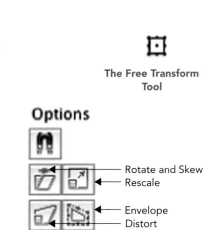

The Free Transform Tool

Options

Rotate and Skew
Rescale
Envelope
Distort

The Free Transform Tool Options

2 When you have the freedom to use all of the options at once, it can be easy to drag in the wrong place and end up with an unexpected result.
Selecting one of the **Free Transform** options limits the transformation to the one you have selected.

3 If you think that you have gone too far with your transformations and want to return to your original version, don't worry, just choose **Modify** > **Transform** > **Remove Transformation** or more simply ⌘/**CTRL** + **SHIFT** + **Z**.

4 As well as altering shapes with the **Free Transform** tool, transformations can be applied numerically in the **Transform** panel. If this panel is not already open, select **Window** > **Design Panels** > **Transform** or more simply ⌘/**CTRL** + **T**.

Rotate and Skew.
SHIFT + drag to rotate
in 45° increments

Rescale. Drag on the corner handles
to rescale proportionally. Drag on the
central handles to squash and stretch

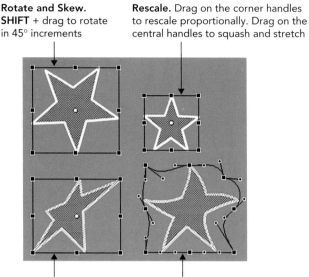

Distort. Drag an edge to distort the shape.
SHIFT + drag on a corner point to taper
the shape. ⌘/**CTRL** + drag on the central
point of an edge allows you to move it freely

Envelope. Allows you to 'warp'
a shape by dragging on the
points and their handles

The Free Transform Options Demonstrated

If this is de-selected, you can
squash and stretch a shape

Select either
Rotate or **Skew**

Creates a transformed copy

Reset to original settings

The Transform Panel

5 The **Modify > Transform** menu also contains the options to **flip horizontal**
and **flip vertical**, which has the effect of mirroring your shape.

Combining Objects

If you are drawing in **Object mode**, as described in Chapter 3, you can take advantage of a new feature in Flash 8, which allows you to combine objects.

Options

Object Mode Selected in Toolbox Options

Select the objects that you want to combine and then **Modify > Combine Objects**. The four options are illustrated below and are useful in enabling you to precisely create complex shapes.

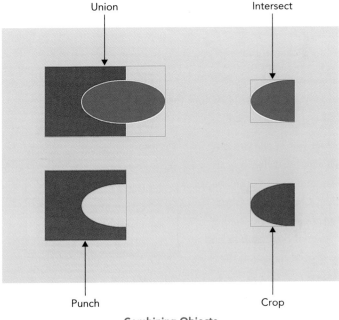

Combining Objects

There are a series of other tools that allow you to modify your drawings in Flash:

Tools for Modifying Drawings

Adding Strokes

The **Ink Bottle** tool allows you to change the thickness, color or style of existing lines (i.e. strokes). You first set up a new line style in the **Properties Inspector** then click on the line you want to change with the **Ink Bottle** tool.

This handy little tool also allows you to add a stroke to filled shapes that have been created without an outline.

Paint Bucket Tool

1 This tool is used to change the color of existing fills, anything created with the **Brush** tool and to fill areas surrounded by lines. Select the color you want to use in the **Fill Color Control** first, then use the **Paint Bucket** tool to click into the area you want to color.

2 Occasionally you may find that this tool just doesn't work. The most common reason for this is that the shape you are trying to color has very small gaps in its outline.

3 Luckily, this tool has a built in **gap size modifier** in case there are gaps in your shape. Select **Close Large Gaps** from these options at the bottom of the **Toolbox** and this should deal with the problem.

Lock Fill

The Paint Bucket Options

4 A common mistake that people make with the **Paint Bucket** tool is to try to use it to color in the background of their image. Remember that the background color is selected in the **Document Properties** and can't be applied with the **Paint Bucket** tool.

Dropper Tool

1 This tool is useful for copying **stroke** and **fill** attributes from other elements. It defaults to either the **Paint Bucket** tool or the **Ink Bottle**

tool depending on whether you have clicked to select a fill or a stroke. You can then take this information and apply it to other fills with the **Paint Bucket** tool or other strokes with the **Ink Bottle** tool.

2 **SHIFT** + click with the **Eyedropper** selects the current color for both the stroke **and** the fill.

Eraser Tool

The **Eraser** tool has a number of options at the bottom of the **Toolbox**. You can choose the shape of the eraser and eraser modes, which are similar to the **Brush** tool modifiers.

Selecting the faucet allows you to click and erase large areas

These are similar to the Brush tool

The Eraser Tool Options

Be careful when using the **Eraser** tool. Double-clicking on the **Eraser** tool icon in the **Toolbox** will delete everything on the Stage.

Rulers, Guides and Grids

1 **Rulers**, **Grids** and **Guides** are useful utilities to aid your drawing process.

2 In order to create **Guides**, first select **View** > **Rulers**. You can then click on your left hand ruler and drag out a vertical guide or drag down a horizontal guide from the top ruler. If you can't see a guide, make sure **View** > **Guides** > **Show Guides** is selected.

3 If you want to permanently remove your guides, choose **View** > **Guides** > **Clear Guides**.

4 Similarly, choose **View** > **Grid** > **Show Grid** to view a grid and **Edit Grid** to change the size of the squares.

5 Grids and guides won't show up in your final movie.

6 Snapping means that there will be a small 'magnetic' pull between what you are drawing or moving and other elements. For example, **View > Snapping > Snap to Grid** means that when you draw near the intersections of the grid a small circle will appear and your shape will snap to that point.

7 **View > Snapping > Edit Snap Align** allows you to alter the snap tolerance. In other words, how close the edge of the object should be to another before it snaps into place.

8 **View > Snapping > Snap Align** – when this is selected, dotted lines appear on the stage when you drag an object to within the specified tolerance. If you drag your shape around the stage, you will see center, top, bottom, left, right alignment lines, depending on where the shape is dragged.

9 **View > Snapping > Snap to Pixels** allows you to snap to a pixel grid, which you can see if the magnification is set to 400% or higher. A useful feature of **Snap to Pixels** is that it can be toggled on/off with a couple of keyboard shortcuts. **C** – turns pixels snapping on or off. **X** – shows or hides the pixel grid.

Pixel Snapping Grid

10 At times **snapping** can be a hindrance and prevent you from drawing exactly where you want to on the stage. If this is this case turn it off by deselecting the various snapping options in the **View** menu.

Step By Step Create a Perspective Grid

1 Turn on **View > Show Grid** and **View > Snapping > Snap to Grid** and **View > Snapping > Snap to Object**.

2 Create a **guide layer**, by clicking on the **Add guide layer** button. Putting your grid on a guide layer means that you won't see it in your final movie.

3 Use the **Line** tool, the **grid** and **snapping** as a reference to build up a perspective grid on this guide layer.

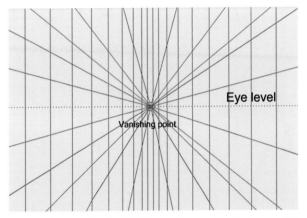

One Point Perspective Grid. This can be used as Reference When You Want to Draw a Scene in Perspective with One Vanishing Point

Using the Grid as Reference

4 Having snapping turned on will enable you to place the origins of your radiating lines exactly on the vanishing points.

5 You can convert a layer into a **guide layer** by **CTRL/RIGHT-clicking** on a layer and then selecting **Guide**.

Converting to a Guide Layer

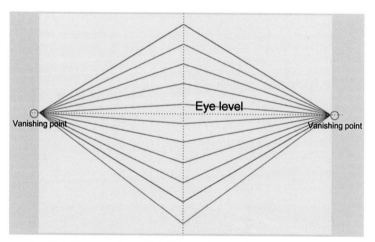

Two Point Perspective Grid. This can be used as Reference When You Want to Draw a Scene in Perspective with Two Vanishing Points

6 When you have drawn your perspective grid, lock this guide layer so that you do not draw on it accidentally. From the options in the Layer window, click in the check box to select **View Layer as Outlines**, so that your grid layer does not become too distracting.

7   You can now use the **Free Transform Tool** to make your drawing work in your chosen perspective view.

8   All that hard work you put into creating a perspective grid can be used again. Select all of your perspective grid and then **Modify** > **Convert to Symbol**. Choose **Graphic** as the symbol type and give it a name that you will remember. You will now be able to recycle this grid many times.

Saving as a Template

9   Another way to recycle your perspective grid is to create a **Template**. Save your Flash document as a template with the perspective grid on a guide layer. Choose **File** > **Save As Template**. Give it a name, a description and either choose from the list of categories or create your own.

Creating a New File from a Template

10 Once you have created a template, you can use it as the basis for a new file. After you have selected **File** > **New**, you are able to choose the **Template** tab and the template you have created will be there available for you to choose.

Drawing Settings

The sensitivity of the drawing and selection tools can be customized in the Flash preferences. To do this on a Mac, go to **Flash** > **Preferences**. To do this on a PC, go to **Edit** > **Preferences**.

How close should the end of a line be to another line before it snaps to connect

How much should curves be smoothed by the smoothing modifier on the Pencil tool

How straight should a Pencil line be before Flash straightens it out

How closely to a shape should you click before it is recognized and corrected

How close must a shape you draw be to a geometric shape before it is recognized and corrected

Flash Preferences

At a Glance Keyboard Shortcuts for the Tools

Keyboard shortcuts are very useful to learn. Not only do they save your time and increase your productivity, but by varying the fingers you are using instead of just holding the mouse, they can help to reduce the chance of repetitive strain injury. Just hit the letter below on your keyboard and you will instantly select the tool.

Keyboard Shortcuts

CHAPTER 5
IMPORTING IMAGES

Vectors vs. Bitmaps

Computers store picture information in two different ways – using **vector** or **bitmap file formats**.

A Vector at Maximum Magnification

A Similar Shape at Maximum Magnification in Bitmap Format

When a **bitmap** file type is used, the computer divides the picture into a grid. You can see the squares on the grid if you zoom in very close to a bitmap image. These squares are known as **pixels**.

Bitmaps are good file types to use when you are working with very complex textures or photographs. However, the file sizes can be large and if your image is scanned or created with a low resolution to keep the file size down, you may get a **pixilated** image in which you can see the square outlines of your pixels.

Vector images, on the other hand, have very small file sizes. The computer uses geometry and mathematics to store the picture information.

Vector files are **resolution independent**. If you zoom in close to them, the outlines will remain crisp and perfect. They are good to use for graphics with blocks of color and gradients, but not so useful for complex textures.

Work produced in vector programs like Flash tend to have a particular 'look' about them. Get some texture into those clean looking vectors with the careful use of bitmaps.

Still Image File Types You Can Import

Although Flash is a fantastic program to use for drawing, you may wish to bring in photographs or other types of images that you have created in software outside Flash. There are many options available to you.

There now follows a list of the main still image file formats that you can import into Flash and some information about them. Check out the Flash **Help** menu if you are interested in importing more specialized file types.

Bitmap File Formats

Name	Details	PC file extension
Bitmap	Although this term denotes a type of file format (e.g. bitmap as opposed to vector), there is also a file format called bitmap or **BMP**. Although it is a standard PC file imaging file format, it can be imported to a Mac using QuickTime.	**.bmp**
EPS	**Encapsulated PostScript** language file format is supported by virtually all graphic, illustration and page-layout programs. It is the most common format for use in desktop publishing. Flash does not, however, support EPS files created from Photoshop.	**.eps**
GIF and animated gif	**Graphics Interchange Format** – commonly used on the web. It produces very small files by reducing the number of colors in your image to a maximum of 256. Consequently, this format is best used for graphics or cartoony type images with areas of flat color. Transparency can be attributed to colors.	**.gif**
JPEG	**Joint Photographic Experts Group** – is commonly used for photographic images. It is a good format for reducing file size while keeping the quality high and commonly used on the web. This format is recommended to bring photographs into Flash, but cannot contain alpha channels.	**.jpg**
Photoshop	The default file format for newly created images in **Photoshop**, which can be imported into Flash if the computer has QuickTime 4 or above loaded. This file format supports all available image modes, guides, alpha channels, spot channels and layers.	**.psd**
PDF	Version 1.4 or above can be imported.	**.pdf**

PICT	A Mac graphical image file format, which can be imported into Flash on a PC if the computer has QuickTime 4 or above loaded.	**.pct**
PNG	**Portable Network Graphics**, a more recent file format used on the web. Can compress to small file sizes while maintaining high quality of image. It supports multiple color depth and grayscales and can contain alpha channel transparency.	**.png**
	PNG is also the standard file format for newly created images in **Fireworks.** See below for more information.	
TGA	**Targa** files can support alpha channel transparency and can be imported into Flash if the computer has QuickTime 4 or above loaded. They are a good choice for exporting in a sequence for output to video.	**.tga**
TIFF	The **Tagged-Image File Format** is usually used for print as it can contain high-resolution data, be in RGB or CMYK or grayscale and can support alpha channel transparency. It can be imported into Flash if your computer has QuickTime 4 or above loaded.	**.tif**

Vector File Formats

Name	Details	PC file extension
Adobe Illustrator files	These files are the standard file format for newly created images in **Illustrator** and can contain layers and guides. Illustrator is an excellent program to create designs for use in Flash. However, there are a few little bugs in the translation between the two programs, so be aware of the following:	**.ai**

- Create the artwork in Illustrator at the size you want to use it in Flash. If you want it smaller, re-scale in Illustrator with the **Scale Strokes and Effects** option selected, then re-import to Flash. This is because line weights rescaling can be unpredictable.
- On import, you can choose to **flatten** all the layers or **convert the layers** into **layers** or **keyframes** in Flash.
- It is best to separate your Illustrator artwork into layers and choose **Layers > Layers** on import. Otherwise, if you create a complicated design in Illustrator all on one layer, Flash may have problems with the stacking order of elements.
- Be careful when using gradient fills. They will be rasterized on import to Flash and lose their vector editability.

- Flash can import files from Illustrator version 10 or earlier, so if you have a more recent version of the program, save as version 10.
- Illustrator objects will be brought in as a group so you will need to **ungroup** them on all layers.
- Illustrator dashed lines and line end caps are not always recognized by Flash. Create plain lines in Illustrator. When you import into Flash ungroup the lines and then add dashes or end caps in the Properties window.

Flash Player	The default file format that is exported from **Flash** to use on the web. You can also import these files into Flash.	.swf
Freehand	Files from **Freehand** version 7 or later can be imported into Flash. Flash supports any layers you may have used in these files. If your Freehand file is in CMYK, Flash will convert it to RGB.	.fh7, .fh8, .fh9, .fh10, .fh11
	As with Illustrator, you can choose to **flatten** all the layers or **convert the layers** into **layers** or **keyframes** in Flash.	
PNG	This file format is also the generic format used by **Fireworks**. If you choose to import a **Fireworks PNG** as a **flattened image**, it will be **rasterized** or converted into a single bitmap image. If you import as an **editable object**, you will maintain the vector artwork.	.png

To Import a Still Image into Flash

1 Make sure the layer you want the image to be on is active.

2 Select **File > Import to Stage**.

3 You can also import numbered sequences of still images. If you do this, the stills will be brought in as successive frames of the layer that is active.

The Library

1 If you can't see the **Library** panel then go to **Window > Library** or ⌘/**CTRL** + **L**. Your image file can be accessed in the **Library**. You can drag further copies of the image on to the Stage from the Library as well as being able to access information about your imported image.

2 The **Library** can also be used to organize your **assets**, that is, any files you have imported or symbols you have created. (More about symbols in the next chapter!) If you click on the **Name** column heading, the files will

The Library

be shown in order of their names. The same will happen for **Type** if you click on that column heading.

3   You can use the **UP** and **DOWN** arrow keys to move up and down in the list of files.

4   If you go to the **Library Options** menu and choose **Edit**, this command launches **Fireworks** or another image editing software package if you don't have Fireworks on your machine. If you select **Edit With**, you can choose which image editing program that you want to use.

Importing Images with Areas of Transparency

If you define an area of transparency using your image-editing software, you maintain this when you import the file into Flash. Here's how to do this using **Photoshop**:

1   In Photoshop, open up the file that you want to create transparency in.

In This File, the Background will be Made Transparent so That Tiggy the Dog Can Be Used in Isolation Without the Foliage in the Background

2   Select the area of the image that you want to use with any combination of selection tools.

Selecting 'Quick Mask' in Photoshop Reveals the Area That Has Been Selected, in This Case, the Dog

3   Go to **Image** > **Image Size** and make a note of the overall pixel dimensions of your image.

```
════════════════════════════ Image Size ═══

┌─ Pixel Dimensions: 1.13M ──────────────────

   Width:  [768        ]  [ pixels ]

   Height: [512        ]  [ pixels ]
```

Image Size Dialogue Box

4   Choose **File** > **New** to start a new file that will be transparent and make sure you have selected **Background** > **Transparent** and **Mode** > **RGB**.

5   The **Resolution** will always be 72 pixels per inch for **screen based** work like that for output to video or the Internet, as this is the resolution of the screen itself.

```
══════════════════════════════ New ═══════════════════════

      Name: [image will have transparent background]    [    OK    ]

   ┌─ Image Size: 1.13M ──────────────────────┐    [  Cancel  ]
   Preset Sizes: [ Custom                  ▲▼ ]

            Width: [768  ]  [ pixels    ▲▼ ]

           Height: [512  ]  [ pixels    ▲▼ ]

       Resolution: [72   ]  [ pixels/inch ▲▼ ]

             Mode: [ RGB Color   ▲▼ ]

   ┌─ Contents ───────────────────────────────
   ○ White
   ○ Background Color
   ◉ Transparent
```

File > New

6 Make this new file exactly the same size as the original image that you first opened.

Drag the Original Image on to the New, Transparent File

7 Using the **Move** tool (shortcut – **V**), drag and drop the image onto the new blank file you created. If you hold down the **SHIFT** key while you drag and drop, the image will be placed in the center of the new file.

8 Close the original file.

Delete the Unwanted Parts of the Image

9   The dog photo now has a transparent background.

10   **File** > **Save** and choose **PNG** as your file format, then **Interlace** > **None**. It is important that you choose **PNG** as the file type, because not all image formats can support transparency.

The Image Without Its Background in Flash

11   **Import** into Flash as above and your image should have a hole in it!

Tracing Bitmaps

If you want to reduce the file size of a bitmap image that you have brought into Flash, you can convert it into a vector graphic.

Another reason for doing this would be to change a photograph into a more stylized vector image:

1   Import the bitmap image file that you want to convert in Flash.

2   Make sure it's selected and then choose **Modify** > **Bitmap** > **Trace Bitmap.**

3 The options that are available are as follows:

- **Color threshold** – Sensitivity of color selection.

- **Minimum area** – The number of surrounding pixels to consider as one block.

- **Curve fit** – How smoothly the outlines will be drawn.

- **Corner fit** – How sharply the edges will be retained.

4 The following settings will give you the best possible settings, however, beware – they might take some time to process depending on the capabilities of your computer. When you trace bitmaps with high quality settings like these it can increase the file size as well as being slow to move around.

Trace Bitmap		
Color threshold:	10	OK
Minimum area:	1 pixels	Cancel
Curve fit:	Pixels	
Corner threshold:	Many corners	

The Best Quality Trace Bitmap Settings

5 Experiment with different settings until you achieve the style that you want. Lower quality settings will take much less time to process.

Two Traced Versions of the Dog Photo with Different Settings Applied. The Middle Version Has Best Quality Settings Applied As Above. The One on the Right *Color Threshold* = 100, *Minimum Area* = 10, *Curve Fit* = Smooth, *Corner Fit* = Normal

6   When you have first completed this process, all the bits of traced bitmap
     will be selected and it will appear to be grayed out.

7   Click away from the image onto a blank part of the Stage to deselect it.

8   You will now be able to adjust individual parts of the image just as if you
     had created the image in Flash with the **Paint** tool.

Painting with Bitmaps

It is possible to import textures and paint with
them in Flash. This can be, especially effective
when used with small tileable textures like
snakeskin or bricks.

1   Import the bitmap you want to use,
     make sure it is selected and **Modify >
     Break apart**.

An Imported PNG file

2   Select the **Eyedropper** Tool and click
     on the broken apart bitmap.

**The Whole of the Traced Dog Was Selected and then Filled with
the Snowflake Image**

3 This loads the image into memory and you can now paint with it using the **Paint** tool. It will also **fill** any shape that you create with the **Pen** tool or the **Oval** or **Rectangle** tools.

4 The **Fill Transform** tool can be used to alter the scale, rotation and skew of the tiled image.

5 You can also select **Bitmap** as a **Fill** option in the **Color Mixer** panel. The bitmap will be tiled to fit the image, as in the image above, and you can adjust it as above with the Fill Transform tool.

Finally, copyright issues don't just apply to music, but also to images. It may be tempting to use other people's images that you have found in books, magazines or on the web, but this is someone else's intellectual property that they have spent time creating. Ultimately, it is much more rewarding to be original and create your own.

CHAPTER 6

LAYERS, SYMBOLS AND KEYFRAMES

Using Layers

Using several layers in Flash allows you to create a complex scene and have more control over your artwork. If you have been drawing in **Merge mode** rather than **Object mode** (cf. Chapter 3), you need to put graphic elements that you want to keep separate on individual layers so they do not merge with the shape underneath.

1   By default there is one layer in your **Timeline**. To create a new layer:
Insert > **Timeline** > **Layer** or more simply click on the **add layer** icon.

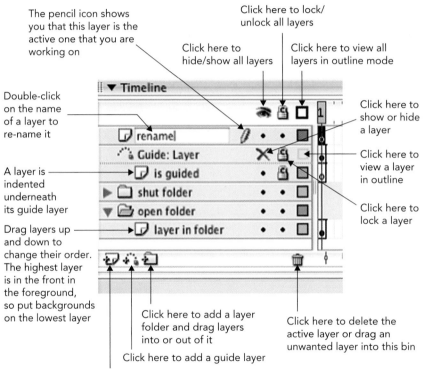

The pencil icon shows you that this layer is the active one that you are working on

Click here to lock/unlock all layers

Click here to hide/show all layers

Click here to view all layers in outline mode

Double-click on the name of a layer to re-name it

Click here to show or hide a layer

A layer is indented underneath its guide layer

Click here to view a layer in outline

Drag layers up and down to change their order. The highest layer is in the front in the foreground, so put backgrounds on the lowest layer

Click here to lock a layer

Click here to add a layer folder and drag layers into or out of it

Click here to delete the active layer or drag an unwanted layer into this bin

Click here to add a guide layer

Click here to add a new layer

Layers

2   Each layer has its own color. This is seen when viewing an anchor point path or when seeing the layer in outline view. You can change this **outline color** so that it contrasts more effectively with the background that you are using. To do this, first select the layer, then

Modify > **Timeline** > **Layer** Properties or more simply **CTRL/ RIGHT-click** on the layer and select **Layer Properties**. The **outline color** can be changed in the window that opens.

Changing the Color of a Layer's Outline In the Layer
Properties Window

3   If you click on a layer's name, you will automatically select all the elements on that layer.

4   Any item that is going to be animated, however small, needs to be on a separate layer, otherwise Flash may not be able to interpret the animation properly.

5   If you have separate elements on one layer that really should be on separate layers, Flash is able to do this automatically for you. Select only the elements that you want to go to new layers and then **Modify** > **Timeline** > **Distribute to Layers**.

Step By Step Create a Manual Drop Shadow

Now, let's look at an example of using layers. Later in the book we'll look at using **Timeline Effects** to automatically create drop shadows. However, creating them manually gives you a lot more control and creativity over the whole process.

1 Duplicate it — ⌘/**CTRL** + **D or SHIFT** + **ALT** + **drag** selection makes a copy with the **Selection** tool.

2 Cut (⌘/**CTRL** + **X**) and paste (⌘/**CTRL** + **V**) and put your shadow on a layer below.

3 While the shape is still selected, change the fill to a dark color and change alpha transparency in the **Color Mixer** panel to a low figure – in this example I used 30%.

Creating a Drop Shadow

4 **Modify** > **Shape** > **Soften Fill Edges** (but beware as this can take time to process and add to the file size in the case of complex shapes). In the example I used a **Distance** of 5 pixels and **Number of steps** – 5. Select your shadow and its new softened edge and **Modify > Group** to keep all the elements together.

Positioning the Drop Shadow

Rotate and Skew Options

5   Examine where the light in your picture is coming from, offset by a few pixels and use the **Rotate** and **Skew** options in the **Free Transform** tool to position your shadow correctly.

Introducing Symbols

1   Flash gives you the capability to go beyond the creation of vector graphics and add the element of interactivity and/or animation to them. One of the ways in which this is done is through the use of **symbols**.

2   A **symbol** is a re-usable object that is saved in the Library panel. You can drag copies of it onto the Stage to use in your movie. A copy

of a symbol used on the Stage is known as an **instance** of the original symbol.

3 There are two ways to create a symbol. As well as creating a symbol from the beginning with **Insert** > **New Symbol** and then creating some artwork, you can also select a piece of artwork on your Stage and choose **Modify** > **Convert to Symbol**.

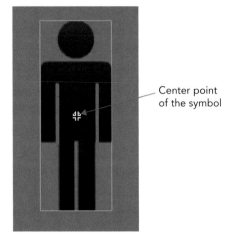

Center point of the symbol

4 You can tell that your artwork has been converted into a symbol because if you select it, it will have a blue bounding box and you can no longer use

A Symbol Has a Blue Bounding Box Around It

the **Eraser**, **Ink Bottle** or **Paint Bucket** tools on it or change the **stroke** and **fill** colors. You can no longer use the **Lasso** or **Subselection** tools to select small sections of this symbol, nor can you reshape the outline with the **Arrow** tool.

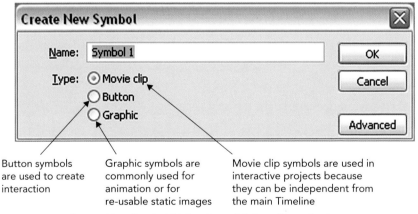

Button symbols are used to create interaction

Graphic symbols are commonly used for animation or for re-usable static images

Movie clip symbols are used in interactive projects because they can be independent from the main Timeline

Create New Symbol Dialog Box with Dropdown Options

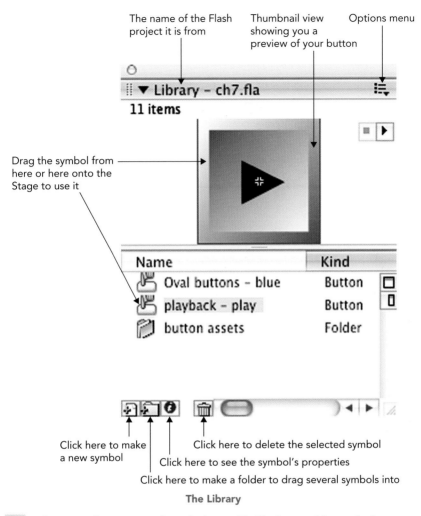

The name of the Flash project it is from

Thumbnail view showing you a preview of your button

Options menu

Drag the symbol from here or here onto the Stage to use it

Click here to make a new symbol

Click here to delete the selected symbol

Click here to see the symbol's properties

Click here to make a folder to drag several symbols into

The Library

5   There are three types of **symbols** used in Flash: **graphic symbols, button symbols** and **movie clip symbols**. Each different type of symbol is described in more detail further on in this book.

6   Although each type of symbol is used for a different purpose in Flash, they all have several things in common:

- each one can be copied many times onto the Stage as an **instance**;

- each one can have its own Stage and its own Timeline.

7   Symbols that you create, as well as bitmaps you have imported, are kept in the Library. If you can't see the Library panel then go to **Window > Library** or ⌘/**CTRL + L**.

8   An individual **instance** (i.e. a copy of the **symbol** that you have dragged from the Library onto the Stage) can be re-colored and made transparent with the **color** options in the Properties Inspector. They can also be rotated and resized with the **Free Transform** tool. These changes to the **instance** on the **Stage** do not alter the **source** symbol in the **Library**.

Interactive Buttons

Now, let's look at one of the types of symbols in more detail.

In Flash, a **Button** is a re-usable **symbol** that can trigger an **action** when it is clicked on. The action could be one of the following:

- start to play or stop a sound;

- jump to another frame;

- play a new scene;

- go to a web site.

Button designs can take different forms. Here are some examples of button design themes:

- **Organizational** – They could relate to the organization of your site and have words on them so that the user is very clear about what the button does.

- **Functional** – They could relate to objects in the real world so that it is clear how they are used, for example looking like a 'play' button or a doorbell.

- **Aesthetic** – Finally, button designs can be taken from the overall design theme and be small versions of a general motif.

If you go to **Window** > **Common Libraries** > **Buttons**, you will find many button files for you to experiment with.

Sample Buttons from the Common Libraries

Creating a Button Symbol

1 Start off by making a new symbol: **Insert** > **New Symbol** and add the settings shown in the diagram below:

```
                    Create New Symbol

   Name:  Button 1                              (  OK  )

 Behavior:   ○ Movie clip                       ( Cancel )
             ◉ Button
             ○ Graphic                          ( Advanced )

            Creating a New Symbol
```

2 The first thing you may notice is that the Timeline looks different and that it says *Scene1 Button1* on the left-hand side of the **Edit Bar**.

77

If you were to click here or there you would be taken
back to Scene1 and, since you haven't placed this
symbol on the Stage yet, the button would disappear

This shows you that you are editing Button1

The four button states

Blank keyframe because
nothing has been created
on the Stage yet

Button Timeline

3   A Button symbol has four frames in its Timeline and they represent the
following states:

- **Frame 1 – UP** = How the button looks when the mouse/cursor is
  no-where near it.

- **Frame 2 – OVER** = How the button looks when the mouse/cursor is
  over it.

- **Frame 3 – DOWN** = How the button looks when it is **clicked** on.

- **Frame 4 – HIT** = The size and shape of the area that will **trigger a
  response** when the mouse/cursor interacts with it. This shape must
  always be a solid filled shape.

4   If all of these four frames are the same, then you have a simple button. If
each frame is different then the button will change with user interaction:
in other words it will be a **rollover** button.

5   You can create **invisible buttons** by only having a solid shape in the
HIT state and nothing in the other three frames. This can be useful for
placing over an illustration to trigger a response.

6   Start off by creating a basic button design in the **Up** frame. The **Up** frame is selected by default, so simply drawing on the Stage will create the first part of this button. The cross hair in the center of the Stage represents the center of the button, so make sure your design takes this into consideration.

The Up frame is created by default   The center of the new button
so creating a button design on the
Stage will create the Up frame

Creating a Basic Button Design

7   In order to change the button **states** in the other three frames you will need to insert a **keyframe** to record the changes between frames. Click in the second – **Over** – frame and choose **Insert** > **Timeline** > **Keyframe**.

8   The **Over** frame is now filled with a black dot showing you that it contains a keyframe. When you first make a keyframe, it is a copy of the last keyframe. Until you make a change on the Stage, the new keyframe has the same contents as the previous keyframe, that is, your **Up** frame button design.

9   Click on the background of the Stage to deselect the shape and then change the color of your button.

10   Repeat the process on the **Down** frame. When a frame is selected, the keyboard shortcut **F6** will also **insert a keyframe** and **F7** will create a **blank keyframe**.

11   Finally, create a keyframe for the **Hit state**, but this time just create a filled solid that will cover the whole area that the user will click on to trigger this button.

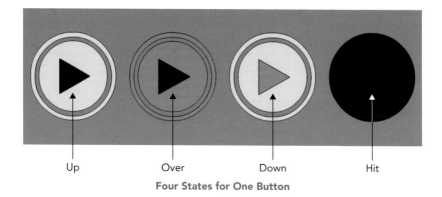

| Up | Over | Down | Hit |

Four States for One Button

12   Exit the Button symbol by clicking on the word Scene1 on the Edit Bar and go back to the main Stage. Make sure that you can see the **Library** panel. Select to **Window** > **Library** or ⌘/**CTRL** + **L** if it is not visible.

Click here to see a quick preview of all four frames

Drag a Copy of the Button onto the Stage

13 Drag a copy of the Button symbol onto the Stage from the Library panel's thumbnail and re-scale it if necessary.

14 Now to preview this button in action, select **Control** > **Enable Simple Buttons**. You are now able to move the mouse/cursor over your button and click on it to see the difference. Deselect **Enable Simple Buttons** when you have finished otherwise you will have problems moving and manipulating your button.

What Is a Keyframe?

Keyframes are used to record changes over time.

The Timeline

When you **insert** a **keyframe**, you actually create a copy of the last keyframe on the layer. The contents can now be either deleted or used as the starting point for new artwork.

This is done by clicking on the Timeline into the frame in which you want to insert a keyframe and then selecting **Insert** > **Timeline** > **Keyframe**. You can also hit **F6** on your keyboard or **CTRL/RIGHT-CLICK** on the frame and select **Insert Keyframe** from the menu.

If, instead, you choose **Insert** > **Timeline** > **Blank Keyframe**, you will insert a **blank keyframe** with nothing on it and you can start a completely new piece of artwork. The shortcut for this is **F7**.

If you want to hold on a keyframe for more than one frame without any changes taking place, then you don't need to insert any more keyframes, but to use **frames** instead. So, frames are used when you want to have a piece of artwork that is not changing at that point in time. To insert frames, click on where you want them to end on the Timeline and then choose **Insert > Timeline > Frame** or hit **F5** on the keyboard.

Naming Symbols

When you create an **instance** of a **symbol**, by dragging a copy of a symbol onto the Stage, it is given a default name by Flash. If you make several copies of one button symbol, you should give each one a name related to its function. This will help you to remember what it does. You can do this in the Properties Inspector.

It is good practice to name all button symbols with the prefix '*btn*' – for example **btnBack** or **btnPlay**. This will help you or any programmers that you may be working with to quickly identify the type of symbol that is being used.

The Properties Inspector When a Button Instance Is Highlighted

Editing Symbols

An instance cannot be modified on the Stage. As mentioned earlier, you can no longer use the **Eraser, Ink Bottle** or **Paint Bucket** tools on it or change the **stroke** and **fill** colors. You can no longer use the **Lasso** or **Subselection** tools to select small sections of this symbol, nor can you reshape the outline with the **Arrow** tool.

However, it is possible to alter the original **symbol** after it has been created. This is done in **Edit Symbol mode**.

There are several ways to enter **Edit Symbol mode**:

- double click the symbol's icon in the Library to open the symbol in isolation;

- select the symbol in the **Library** panel and then **Edit** from the **Options menu** at the top right-hand side;

- double click the symbol on the Stage to edit it in the context of the rest of your design on the Stage. This is a shortcut for **Edit > Edit in Place**, which allows you to see your scene in the background while you are editing.

To exit **Edit Symbol mode**, click on the word Scene1 on the left of the **Edit Bar** above the Stage to go back to the main Stage. You could also click on the **Back** button at the left of the **Edit bar** or choose **Select Edit > Edit Document**.

After you have edited a symbol, all of its instances that have been copied onto the Stage will change too.

If you want to keep your original symbol intact and create another version of it, you can **duplicate** a symbol by choosing **Modify > Symbol > Duplicate Symbol** and then alter the duplicate.

What Is a Behavior?

Interactivity is created in Flash using a language called **ActionScript**. This can be complicated to learn and so Macromedia have provided a number of pre-written scripts called **behaviors** for beginners or those with a phobia for programming.

Event	Action
On Release	Go to Web Page...

Click here to add a behavior — This shows you the name of your button and the symbol it came from — This is the behavior that is applied to this button

The Behaviors Panel

If you can't see the **Behavior** panel, go to **Window > Behaviors**.

Step By Step Create a Links Page

In this exercise, we will create a Links page for a web site.

1   Follow the steps earlier in this chapter to create a button symbol or use one of the designs that come with Flash in **Window > Common Libraries > Buttons**.

2   Drag a copy from the Library onto the Stage.

3   Hold down the **ALT** key and drag on the button to create copies of it. Make a button for each link you want to use. Place them on the left-hand side of the Stage in a vertical line.

4   Select all of the buttons and use the **Align** panel to space them equally. If you can't see the **Align** panel, go to **Window Align** or more simply ⌘/CTRL + K.

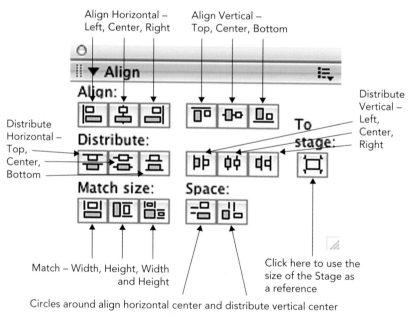

Align Horizontal –
Left, Center, Right

Align Vertical –
Top, Center, Bottom

Distribute
Horizontal –
Top,
Center,
Bottom

Distribute
Vertical –
Left,
Center,
Right

Match – Width, Height, Width
and Height

Click here to use the
size of the Stage as
a reference

Circles around align horizontal center and distribute vertical center

The Align Panel

5 Making sure **To Stage** is **not** selected, click on **align horizontal center** and **distribute vertical center**. Your buttons should now be perfectly positioned. Click on the background of the Stage to de-select them.

Name Each Button

6 Select the first button that you want to add a link to and give it a **name** that will remind you of its function in the Properties Inspector.

7 Open the **Behavior** panel, if you can't see it, go to **Window** > **Behaviors**. Click on the plus sign to add a behavior and choose **Web** > **Go to Web Page**.

Click here to add a behavior

Behavior

Add the full address here

How the new page will open:

_self = will open in the current window and your web site will be closed.

_blank = will open in a new window so that your web site will still be open in a window underneath.

_parent = if you have frames in your web site then the new page will open in the parent frame.

_top = if you have frames in your web site then the new page will open in the top-level frame of the current window.

Go to URL

8 Type in the full address of the link you want to open. You can copy and paste this information from the address bar of your favorite Internet browser.

9 .html is the file extension for a **HTML** page commonly exported by a Mac. **.htm** is the same file type, but this extension is more commonly used with the Windows system. Both extensions can be read by both platforms, so this is a minor detail. However, in web design you must be 100% accurate when using file names to link to other pages, so whichever you use, be consistent.

10 Choose **Open in** > **_blank** so that your web site will still be open on the users computer.

11 Select each button in turn and repeat the process until each one has a **Go to Web Page** behavior attached to it.

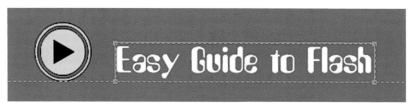

Using Snap Align to Position Text Next to the Buttons

12 Create text for the page and, making sure that **View** > **Snapping** > **Snap Align** is selected, move it around the page and use the guide to align the text with the buttons.

13 Create other design elements to make your links page look exciting. Make sure you are regularly saving this Flash project.

14 Now to test it. Go to **Control** > **Test Movie**. This creates a test version of your movie in the form of a .SWF file. It will be named after the name that you have given the project and will be saved in the same folder in which you have saved your project. Even though this is only supposed to be a test version, it is in the correct format to put straight into a HTML page and go live on the Internet. We will look at this process in more detail in Chapter 14.

As well as adding links to buttons, it is very straightforward to add a URL to text in Flash. It is done at the bottom of the Properties Inspector.

Add the full URL to   Select the link   Click on the triangle
your link here   target here   to expand this
                                                       window if you can't
                                                       see the links boxes

The Properties Inspector

Select some text to add a link to and type in the full address in the **URL link box** in the Properties Inspector.

Text with a Link Applied Has a Dotted Line Underneath

Using Movie Clip Symbols

In addition to **button symbols**, there is a second type of symbol called a **movie clip symbol**. These are like Flash movies within Flash movies with their own layers and timelines. They are independent of the main Timeline, for example, they could be triggered by a user interaction like clicking on a button.

Movie clip symbols can be thought of as rebellious symbols that refuse to conform to the rules of the Timeline they are placed in.

We will now look at using movie clip symbols to create a button that animates when you hold the mouse over it.

Step-By-Step Animated Rollover Buttons

1 First of all we will create a small piece of animation inside a movie clip. Go to **Insert > New Symbol,** or use the keyboard shortcut – ⌘/**CTRL + F8,** then choose **Movie Clip** as the **behavior** and give it a name that will remind you of its content.

2 It is best practice to name your movie clip symbols using the prefix '*mc*', for example *mcArrows*. Using a consistent convention like this will make sure that all of your movie clips will be grouped together in your library and will make any programmer that you are working with happy.

Create New Symbol	
Name: mcArrows	OK
Behavior: ◉ Movie clip	Cancel
○ Button	
○ Graphic	Advanced

Creating a Movie Clip

3 Create a basic button shape. Name the layer after the type of shape you have created and **lock** this layer.

4 Add a second layer, make sure it is the top layer and create a small triangle on it in a contrasting color. Name this layer '*triangle*'.

5 The idea now is to create a small animation of this triangle moving across the button shape that can loop endlessly over 10 frames.

▼ Timeline

Extend the Button Shape Layer By 10 Frames

6 The overall button shape itself will not be moving, so its layer does not require any further keyframes. However, we do want to see it for the whole 10 frames so will need to **insert frames**. Click in frame 10 of the button shape layer and select **Insert > Timeline > Frame** or more simply F5, so that your button shape layer now lasts for 10 frames.

7 Click in frame 10 of the *triangle* layer and select **Insert > Timeline >** **Keyframe** or more simply **F6** to insert a keyframe. By inserting a keyframe in frame 10, there are now two identical keyframes on frames 1 and 10, so the start and end of this animation is the same.

8 Click in frame 2 of the *triangle* layer and **insert a keyframe**. The triangle shape is selected by default so just use the **RIGHT** arrow key on your keyboard to nudge it along to the right.

| Frame 1 | Frame 2 | Frame 4 | Frame 6 | Frame 8 | Frame 10 |

Moving the Triangle

9 **Insert a keyframe** in frame 4, nudge the triangle further along until its center is in line with the edge. Use the **Selection** tool (**V**) to drag out a marquee and select the overlapping excess that is outside the button's outline. Drag that piece over to the left-hand edge of the button shape.

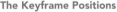

The Keyframe Positions

10 On frame 6, insert a keyframe and align the triangle with the left edge. On frame 8, insert a keyframe and nudge the triangle further to the right.

11 In order to preview how this will look when it is looping, select **Control** > **Loop Playback** and then hit the **RETURN/ENTER** key to play. To stop it playing, hit **RETURN/ENTER** a second time.

12 This **movie clip symbol** is going to be placed within a **button symbol** to create an animated rollover button. However, first, in order to maintain continuity in the overall button shape and color, go to frame 1 and unlock the button shape layer. Now select both the triangle and the button shape and **Edit** > **Copy**.

Create a Button Symbol

13   Go to **Insert > New Symbol**, choose **Button** as the **behavior** and give it a name that will remind you of its content.

14   Click in the **Up** frame and select **Edit > Paste in Place**. Next select the third **Down** frame and **insert a keyframe**. De-select by clicking on the background of the Stage and change the color of the triangle to match the background of your Stage.

15   Make sure that your **Library** panel is open. Click in the second Over frame and **insert** a **blank keyframe**. Drag your **movie clip symbol** onto the Stage from the **preview thumbnail** in the **Library**.

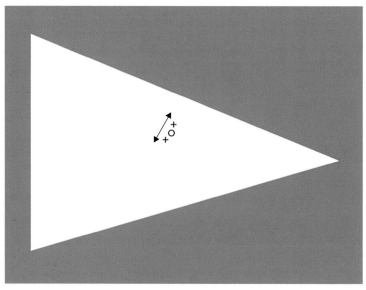

Aligning the Crosshairs

16   Zoom in and use the arrow keys on your keyboard to make sure that the movie clip's central crosshair is exactly over the central crosshair of the button symbol.

17   **Insert a keyframe** into the fourth **Hit** frame and while the whole shape is selected, choose black as the color for both the **fill** and **stroke color controls**. The whole of the button should be a solid black color now.

18   Click on **Scene1** in the **Edit Bar** to return to the main Stage. Drag a copy of the **button symbol** that you have just created out of the Library and onto the Stage.

19   Select **Control > Test Movie** to preview your button in action. You can exit from the **Test Movie** window by clicking on the **X** in the top corner of this window – just as you would to close a window in any other program.

You could also apply a behavior to this button now, just like earlier in this chapter.

Filters and Blends

If you have purchased a copy of Flash 8 Professional, you will be able to apply **Filters** and **Blends** to **Movie Clip** and **Button** symbols. **Filters** can also be applied to **text**. These are new features, so in order

▼   Properties   Filters

The Filters Tab

to use them your document will need to be set to publish for Flash Player 8, as described in Chapter 3.

Filters can be accessed by clicking on the tab behind the **Properties Inspector**.

Once selected, filter options will become available in the Properties window. Experiment until you achieve your required effect.

Blend modes can be selected from the dropdown menu in the Properties window. Just as with **Filters**, these are Flash 8 Professional features that can be applied to **Movie Clip** and **Button** symbols. In addition, they can only be used

Click on the + sign to add a filter to selected text, button or movie clip

The Filters

Blend Modes are Accessed from the Properties Window

in documents that will be published to Flash Player 8. If Flash Player 8 is not selected in the Publish Settings, you will get the following error message:

Flash 8 ⊠

⚠ This feature is not supported by Flash Player 7. To use this feature, you must target Flash Player 8.

Publish Settings...   OK

Flash Player Compatibility Error Message

Blend modes are a way of combining the colors, brightness and darkness values of overlapping **Movie Clip** and **Button** symbols.

Blend Modes Applied to Movie Clip Symbols

CHAPTER 7

MENU NAVIGATION

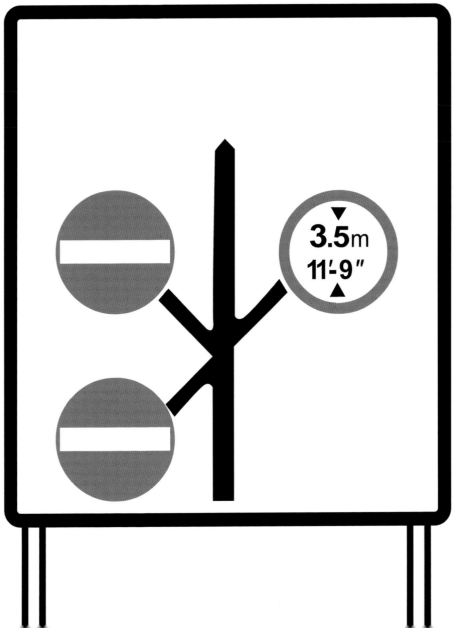

In this chapter we will look at creating more complex navigation through using buttons in groups as menus, through the use of movie clip symbols and by creating submenus.

Button Actions and Frame Actions

For people who are learning Flash or are scared of ActionScript, Macromedia have provided not only **Behaviors** – complete mini scripts that you can customize as we saw in the last chapter, but also **Actions** – pre-written pieces of code that you can combine and customize for your own requirements.

Actions can be attached to frames as well as to buttons, for example to pause on a frame or for making a new movie load on a particular frame or to loop a sequence.

In the last chapter we saw that **movie clip** symbols could be contained within **button** symbols to create animated rollovers. **Frame actions** can also be contained within symbols to create a more complex piece. **Button** symbols can also be placed within **movie clip** symbols. However, you cannot put **button symbols** within **button symbols**.

We will now look at creating a simple menu using frame actions and behaviors.

Creating a Basic Menu

A menu often consists of a series of buttons that are all based on the same design with text labels to describe their different functions. In this case, you only need to create one button symbol for all of the buttons. The text for the buttons can be placed on a layer above.

The menu in this example has three buttons linked to three frames. When you click on a button you jump to the associated frame. The text in the button changed color when you are on the frame that the button links to.

1   Follow the steps given in Chapter 6 to create a simple button and call it **btnNumbers**. Drag a copy onto the Stage.

2   Hold down the **ALT** key and drag out two copies of this button. Use the **Align** panel to make sure that they are evenly spaced.

3 Name this layer '*buttons*' and then lock the *buttons* layer.

4 Make a second layer above by selecting **Insert** > **Timeline** > **Layer** or click on + icon underneath the layer names. Name this layer '*button text*' as it will be used to create the text for the buttons on.

5 Using the **same** color as your background, type the word **HOME** and position it over the first button. Using a **contrasting** color, type the word **HOME** again, make the font size very large and position this on the other side of your page.

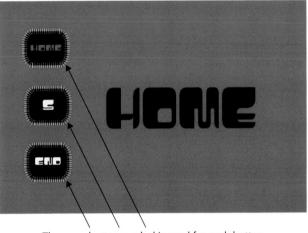

The same button symbol is used for each button, only the text on the layer above changes

The First Frame

6 Using another **contrasting** color, type in **5** and then the word **END**. Place each of these over the other two buttons.

7 The text is going to change in color over time depending on which frame you are on, but the basic background button shape will not, so the *buttons* layer just needs frames – not keyframes. Click on frame 10 of the *buttons* layer and **F5** to **insert frames**.

8 **Insert a keyframe** on frame 5 of the *button text* layer. Delete the word **HOME** on the right side of the Stage and add a **5**. Change the button text colors as per the diagram above.

Frame 5

Frame 10

9   **Insert a keyframe** on frame 10 of the ***button text*** layer. Delete **5**, add **END** and change the button text colors as per the diagram above.

10   Now lock the ***button text*** layer so that you do not alter it by accident.

11   Select the **home** button and name it ***btnHome*** in the Properties Inspector. Open the **Behavior** panel – **Window** > **Behaviors** or **SHIFT** + **F3**.

Goto and Stop Behavior

12 In the **Behavior** panel, click on the + sign to add a behavior and choose **Movieclip** > **Goto and Stop at frame or label**.

Goto and Stop on Frame 1

13 Make sure you have all of the same settings as the diagram above. This means that when you click on this button, it will take you to frame 1.

14 Select the 5 button next, name it **btn5** in the Properties Inspector and add the **goto and stop at frame or label** behavior to it as before.

Goto and Stop at frame or label

Choose the movie clip that you want to stop playing:

this

🖼 _root

⦿ Relative   ○ Absolute

Enter the frame number or frame label at which the movie clip should stop playing:

5

Cancel   OK

Goto and Stop on Frame 5

15 Make sure you have all of the same settings as the diagram above. This button will take you to frame 5.

16 As well as using this behavior to go to a frame number, you can also name a frame with a label and choose to go to the frame label. This is especially useful if you have a complicated site with lots of frames.

17 Add another layer and call it *labels&actions*. Click in frame 10, **insert a blank keyframe** and type **end** in the Properties Inspector to name this frame.

Frame

end

Type 'end' in the Properties Inspector

18 Select the **End** button next, name it *btnEnd* in the Properties Inspector and add the **go to and stop at frame or label** behavior to it as before.

19 Make sure you have all of the same settings as the diagram next page. This button will take you to the frame called '**end**'.

20 **Control > Test movie** to test out your project so far. Did you spot the deliberate mistake? The test movie is looping through the frames instead of starting out with a static frame. This can be corrected by the use of a frame action-making the movie pause on the first frame.

Goto and Stop at frame or label

Choose the movie clip that you want to stop playing:

> this
>
> 📖 _root

○ Relative   ○ Absolute

Enter the frame number or frame label at which the movie clip

should stop playing:

> end

Cancel   OK

Goto and Stop on Frame 'end'

Actions and Script Assist

Sound: None ⊕

Effect: None   Edit...

Click here in the Properties
window to open the Actions panel

21 Click in frame 1 of the *labels&actions* layer to select it and then click on
the small, circled arrow in the Properties Inspector to open the Actions

▼ Actions - Frame

ActionScript 1.0 & 2.0

📘 Global Functions
 ↗ Timeline Control
 ↗ Browser/Network
 ↗ Printing Functions
 ↗ Miscellaneous Functions
 ↗ Mathematical Functions
 ↗ Conversion Functions
 ↗ Movie Clip Control

Script Assist

1

Click to make Script Assist   Select Script Assist
active List of Actions

A Select Script Assist

panel. You can also open this panel by **Window** > **Actions**. Don't feel intimidated by this panel, you really do not need to know everything it contains at this stage.

22   Script Assist helps you to build scripts by selecting items from the list of Actions on the left-hand side.

The Stop Action

23   Click on the folder **Global Functions** to open it and then on the folder **Timeline Control** to open that. Finally, double-click on the action '**stop**' to apply it to this frame.

24   The **Options** menu in the **Actions** Panel contains **View Esc Shortcut Keys**. If you select this option you will see shortcuts beside the different functions on the left-hand side.

25   A handy little shortcut if this option is selected – when the Actions window is open, pressing **ESCAPE** on your keyboard then **S** then **T** will add the **Stop** action.

26   **Control** > **Test** movie to test out your project again. This time the buttons all work and the movie stops on the frame it is supposed to stop on.

Create an Online Portfolio

At times, you may wish to navigate through categories of information rather than simple links. In the following example of an online portfolio, the first menu that you come to is a pop-up menu. In other words, when you click on a button you are not taken straight to a frame, but given the choice of further buttons to click on.

An online portfolio is an excellent way to showcase your work. It should be easy to access information on it and for clients to view examples of your work.

Menus and Submenus

The following exercise will allow you to create a pop-up menu for an online portfolio with four basic sections:

- **home** – on which your contact details are shown,

- **gallery** – from which you can view images,

- **about** – which contains text about yourself,

- **links** – a selection of your favorite links.

Each of these basic sections can be divided into further categories or '*submenus*'. Create your own design concept and customize this basic structure to suit your own needs.

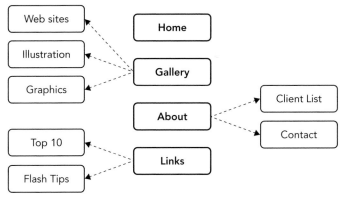

The Menu and Submenus in this Example

Create a Pop-up Menu in a Movie Clip

1 First of all, decide on the size that your overall site will have and the color scheme that you will be using and **modify** your **document** accordingly.

2 The aim is to create a site with a pop-up menu – a menu in which subcategories pop-up when you click on one of the main buttons. This whole menu will be placed in a movie clip symbol, because this will enable it to control events on the Stage whilst remaining independent.

The Top Level of the Menu

3 First create a movie clip in which the whole pop-up menu system will be contained: **Insert** > **New Symbol** > **Movie Clip** and call it *'mcMenu'*.

4 Next create the generic buttons which will be used in the menu. Text will be added to them on the Stage later, so do not create any text within the button at this point.

5 **Insert** > **New Symbol** > **Button** and call it *'btnMain'*. Design the **Up** frame for a plain button, **without any text**, which will be for the four main sections or the *top level* of your menu. Keep it simple at the stage – you could always go back and edit it at a later date.

6 Now create the **Over** and **Hit** frames. Do this by adding a keyframe to the **Over** and **Hit** frames. Then modify the graphic in the **Over** frame. Remember that the **Hit** frame only needs a filled solid shape as all it is doing is defining the area to respond to a mouse click. You don't need to add a **Down** state for this button.

Generic Main Menu Button – *'btnMain'* – and Generic Submenu Button – *'btnSub'*

7 Next, create another **plain** button, which we will use for the items in the **submenu** that you will see when you hold the mouse over one of the main buttons. To maintain design continuity, make this button similar in some way to the previous button. Call it '**btnSub**'. As you have already done add the **Over**, also the **Down** and **Hit** frames.

8 You should still be within the **mcMenu** movie clip. Rename **layer 1** as '**main buttons**'. This is the layer on which the four main section buttons will be placed. Drag a copy of the **btnMain** button out of the Library.

9 Hold down the **ALT** key and drag out three copies. Position all four buttons in a row at the left of your Stage and use the **Align** panel to make sure that they are equally spaced.

10 Next create a new layer and call it '**button text**'. As in the exercise before, create the text for your four buttons – **HOME, GALLERY, ABOUT** and **LINKS** and place it on top as in the diagram above.

The Four Main Buttons with Text Placed on a Layer Above

The Sub Level of the Menu

11 Next we will create the submenu – the buttons that you will see when you hold the mouse over one of the main buttons.

12 Create two more layers and name them '**labels&actions**' and '**sub buttons**'. Make sure that they are in the order shown in the diagram above.

Layer Order

13 Click in frame 30 of the **main buttons** layer and press **F5** to create frames. These buttons will not be changing so you do not need to add keyframes on this layer. Lock this layer so that you don't move the buttons around by mistake.

14 As in the previous exercise put a **Stop** action into frame 1 of the **labels&actions** layer.

Click in Frame 1 and Add the Following from the Actions Panel

15 Now select frame 10 of the top three layers only and **insert a keyframe**. Click into this keyframe for the *labels&actions* layer and name the frame '*gallery*' in the Properties Inspector.

Frame

gallery

Naming the Frame

16 Now click on the **sub buttons**, layer so that it is the active layer, and drag in a button for each type of work that you do.

The Gallery Submenu   The About Submenu   The Links Submenu

17 Add text for each of these new buttons in the **button text** layer and change the color of the **GALLERY** text.

18 Add keyframes on the top three layers on frame 20. Repeat the process above naming the frame on the *labels&actions* layer '*about*' and creating categories about yourself.

19 Add keyframes on the top three layers on frame 30. Repeat the process above naming the frame on the **labels&actions** layer '**links**' and creating categories for your links. Add five more blank frames after '**links**' so you can see the label.

The Layers and Labels

Buttons as Menus

20 We have added the basic buttons – the next step is to make them actually work. Go back to frame 1. Unlock the **btnMain** layer and lock the other three layers.

21 Select the **HOME** button. Name it **btnHome** in the Properties inspector and select the **track as menu item** option. This allows the buttons to act as a group. It means other buttons can receive mouse event information.

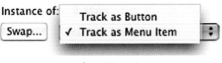

Track as Menu Item

22 As in the previous exercise, click on the **plus** sign in the behaviors panel and choose **Movieclip > Goto and Stop at frame or label** to apply this behavior. Make sure (**'mcMenu'**) is selected as the **movie clip** and it says **1** in the frame number/label field.

The Mouse Event Types

23 Click on the **mouse event type** in the **Behaviors** panel and select **On Roll Over**. This means that the user will be taken to the new frame when they hold the mouse over this button. They will not need to click on the button to activate it.

24 Select the **GALLERY, ABOUT** and **LINKS** buttons in turn and name each one in turn in the Properties Inspector as *btnGallery, btnAbout* and *btnLinks*. Then make sure that **track as menu item** is selected for each one.

25 Finally, apply the **Goto and Stop at frame or label** behavior to each one, making sure that the **GALLERY** button is going to the **gallery** frame label, the **ABOUT** button is going to the **about** frame label and the **LINKS** button is going to the **links** frame label.

Goto and Stop at frame or label

Choose the movie clip that you want to stop playing:

this

▼ _root
(menu)

⊙ Relative   ○ Absolute

Enter the frame number or frame label at which the movie clip should stop playing:

gallery

Cancel   OK

Goto and Stop Behavior Applied to the Gallery Button

26 Select **On Roll Over** for each button.

27 Click on **scene 1** in the Edit Bar to go back to the main Stage and out of the *mcMenu* movie clip. Drag a copy of this *mcMenu* movie clip out of the **Library** and onto the **Stage**.

Name the Movie Clip

28 Name the layer that the menu movie clip is on '**menu**'.

29 In the Properties Inspector, name this movie clip '**mcMainmenu**'. **Control >
Test Movie** to look at this menu so far.

Controlling Events on the Stage

In the previous exercise, you completed a menu system that was completely
contained within a movie clip.

Once this menu movie clip is on the Stage, you can use it to control events on
the Stage:

1 In the Timeline for the main scene, create a '**labels&actions**' layer.
Place new blank keyframes with labels at regular intervals for every
single submenu item.

Target Frames for the Submenu Buttons

2 Following on from the menu system created in the previous example,
create labeled keyframes for all of the following:

- home,
- web sites,
- illustration,
- graphics,
- client list,
- contact,
- top 10,
- flash tips.

3 Add content to each of these frames for the submenu buttons to link to.

But how do you connect the buttons *Within* the movie clip menu to labeled frames on the *Stage*? Don't they have different timelines?

4 **Double-click** on your **menu** movie clip on the Stage to open it in **Edit Symbol** mode.

5 Select the button in your menu that you want to link to a frame on the main Stage. Add the **Goto and Stop behavior** to it.

Goto and Stop at frame or label

Choose the movie clip that you want to stop playing:

```
this._parent
```

▼ 🖼 _root
   🖼 mainmenu

⦿ Relative   ◯ Absolute

Enter the frame number or frame label at which the movie clip should stop playing:

```
home
```

(Cancel) (OK)

Linking a Button Within a Movie Clip Menu to Open a Frame on the Main Stage

---

6 Make sure **_root** is selected as the movie clip and type in the name of the frame. This means that you will go to that frame on the main Stage rather than a frame in the movie clip symbol itself.

7 Carry on linking all of the buttons to the frames that you have created content on and labeled.

Loading Images

If you were to create a Flash movie and put lots of jpeg images in it, you could end up with a very large file size and clients may not have the patience to wait for it to download. So instead of **embedding** images within this site, we are going to look at using buttons and behaviors to **load** an external image into a target on your page.

1 In order for this to work simply, all your images must be **jpegs** that you have previously optimized and cropped to the **same size** as your **target** using an Image Editing program like Fireworks or Photoshop. In this example, the target and the image sizes are all 390 × 290 pixels, but this will vary according to your design.

2 Another way to keep this whole process very simple is to make sure that all of your jpegs are in the **same folder** as your Flash project and final Flash movie.

3 Next create a new movie clip symbol, which is a simple rectangle and call it '*mcTarget*'.

The Image Target and Buttons

4 Make sure that the top left-hand corner of the rectangle snaps onto the crosshair in the center point of the symbol. If you do not do this then your image will not load correctly.

5 Then drag a copy of '*mcTarget*' into your main movie. You can check the pixel dimensions of this movie clip in the **Info** panel –⌘/**CTRL** + I if you can't see it.

Align the Top-left Corner of the Rectangle with the Center Point of the Symbol

6 Select the *mcTarget* movie clip and name it '*mcImage_target*' in the Properties Inspector. Then select **Alpha** from the **color pop-up** in the Properties Inspector and set this to 0% to make it transparent.

The Properties Inspector for the Movie Clip

7 Next create a series of buttons, each of which is going to open up a new image into the '*mcImage_target*' movie clip.

The Load Graphic Behavior

8 Select the first of the image buttons. Give each one its own name in the Properties Inspector. Add the behavior **Movieclip** > **Load Graphic** to each button and the file name of the image that you want it to load.

Load Graphic

Enter the URL to the .JPG to load:

myimage.jpg

Select the movie clip into which to load the graphic:

this.mcImage_target

🖼 _root

   🖼 mcImage_target

◉ Relative   ◯ Absolute

The Load Graphic Window

9 Make sure that *mcImage_target* is selected as the movie clip into which to load the graphic. Remember that your jpeg file *must* be in the same folder as your Flash project for this to work.

10 We will also need to make sure that each time you load a graphic, you close the one that was previously opened, so we will need to add a second action to each of the image buttons as below.

▼ Behaviors

🔲 ⊖ 🗊   B image <B 1>   △ ▽

Data ▶
Embedded Video ▶
Media ▶
Movieclip ▶
Projector ▶
Sound ▶
Web ▶

Bring Forward
Bring to Front
Duplicate Movieclip
Goto and Play at frame or label
Goto and Stop at frame or label
Load External Movieclip
Load Graphic
Send Backward
Send to Back
Start Dragging Movieclip
Stop Dragging Movieclip
Unload Movieclip

The Unload Movie Behavior

11 Select *mcImage_target* as below.

Unload Movieclip

Select the movie clip to unload:

this.mcImage_target

_root

mcImage_target

○ Relative ○ Absolute

The Unload Movie Window

12 We just need to alter the order of these two behaviors now, so that the previous image is unloaded before the new image is loaded.

▼ Behaviors

B_image, <B_1>

Event	Action
On Release	Load Graphic...
On Release	Unload Movieclip...

With the Unload Behavior Selected, click on this Triangle to Alter the Order

▼ Behaviors

B_image, <B_1>

Event	Action
On Release	Unload Movieclip...
On Release	Load Graphic...

The Behavior Order is Now Changed

13 Make sure that you are saving regularly!

Mail to Link

Finally, after all of your hard work, you will want people to be able to contact you through your web site. This can be done through a text link or a button using 'mail to'. When this type of link is clicked on, the users email program will open on their computer and they will be able to send you an email directly.

Adding Mail to (Circled)

To add a *'mail to'* to text, highlight the text you want to add this link to and add **mailto**: followed by your full email address in the **URL links** box in the Properties Inspector as below.

Go to URL

URL: `mailto:me@focalpress.com`

Open in: `"_blank"`

Cancel   OK

Adding a Mail to Goto URL

In order to attach a *'mail to'* to a button, use the **Goto URL behavior** and type the text in exactly as above.

Submit Your Portfolio

If you have successfully completed an online portfolio that you are proud of, contact us at **www.easyguidetoflash.com** and submit a link to your URL so that other readers can view your work.

CHAPTER 8
ANIMATION

Animation is the illusion of movement caused by a sequence of pictures changing rapidly over time. Due to a process known as the 'persistence of vision' our eyes are tricked into seeing these still images as being in motion rather than as individual pictures.

To create animation with Flash you also create a series of still images – on the Stage – and change them over time to give the impression of movement. A change is recorded by a **keyframe**, so each time you move, redraw, rotate etc your drawings on the Stage you will need to create a **keyframe** to save all the different drawings in your sequence. You will then be able to play them back and see your drawings come to life.

There are two different ways to produce animation in Flash. The first is very intuitive. **Frame-by-frame animation** involves drawing each frame individually. In terms of traditional animation, this is like using Flash as your line tester. The second method may seem more complex, but once you have grasped the concepts of animating with **tweening** you will be able to save yourself a lot of time.

Creating a Banner Ad with Frame-By-Frame Animation

Frame-by-frame animation is the easiest way to animate in Flash.
The first stage is to create the artwork that you want to animate.

Creating a Document for a Web Banner with a Template

You then separate the different elements onto different layers.

1   Start a new Flash Project. **Modify** your **document** so that it is 468 × 60 pixels in size with a frame rate of 12 frames per second.

2   A quicker way to do this is to choose **File** > **New** > **Template** > **Advertising** > **468 × 60 Banner**.

3   A good length for a banner ad is 3 seconds, so try to keep all your animation within a duration of 36 frames.

Design a Background for Your Animation

4   Experimenting with the different drawing tools and the marks they make, design a background – either a landscape or a pattern, which will not be animated. Name this layer **background** by clicking twice on the existing layer name. Lock this layer if you do not want to change it again.

Separating and Locking Layers

5   Make a new layer by selecting **Insert** > **Layer** or by clicking on the + icon at the bottom left of the Timeline.

6   Draw a character or shape or text to be animated on this new layer and name the layer appropriately so that it is easy for you to remember what is on each layer.

7   You could also import bitmaps onto different frames and move them around.

The Layer that is at the Top of the Stack of Layers in Your Timeline will be in the Foreground of your Animation. The Bottom Layer will be in the Background

8 If you have several elements on one layer, you can get Flash to automatically put them on separate layers by first selecting the layer and all it's contents and then the command **Modify** > **Distribute to Layers**.

9 Remember **Merge drawing** and **Object drawing** from Chapter 3? If your shapes have been drawn in **merge** mode and they overlap, they will not be put on separate layers, but thought of as one element.

10 To re-order the layers you just need to click onto the name of the layer and drag it either up or down.

Using Keyframes to Record Animation

11 The next stage is to get your artwork moving. In order to do frame-by-frame animation, you'll need to remember to **insert** a new **keyframe** every time you make a change to your artwork on the Stage.

An Expanded View of a Frame-By-Frame Animation of a Bird

12 Move ahead in the Timeline by 1 or 2 frames, click on a keyframe to select it and **Insert** > **Timeline** > **Keyframe** or **F6** for the layer that you want to animate. This will copy the keyframe before and you can now alter it.

13 If you choose **Insert** > **Timeline** > **Blank Keyframe** or **F7**, you will insert a totally blank keyframe and you can draw from scratch.

Keyframe   Blank Keyframe

Altering Keyframe

14 The amount of keyframes that are used will affect the smoothness of your action. If you want your action to be fast and smooth – put a keyframe on every frame. For normal action you can probably get away with putting a keyframe on every other frame.

Create a New Keyframe for Each New Drawing

15 When you see a black dot on the Timeline you know you have a keyframe. However, if you have a complicated scene you may not remember what is on each keyframe. There is a way, though, to get a look at the contents of your keyframe. At the end of your Timeline is a **Frame View button**.

Tiny
Small
✓ Normal
Medium
Large

Short

✓ Tinted Frames

Preview
Preview In Context

The Frame View Button at the End of the Timeline

16 If you click on this button, you have some options as to how to view your frames. You can alter the size that they are displayed on the Timeline and you can also choose **Preview** and **Preview in Context**.

Preview Shows Only What is on the Layer – Not Any Surrounding Empty Space.
Preview in Context Shows What is on the Layer in Proportion to the Whole Stage

Onion Skinning

17 You may want to be able to refer to keyframes before and after the point in time that you are working on. You can do this by using **onion skinning**.

18 **Onion skinning** is turned on and off by selecting the little buttons at the bottom of the Timeline. You can choose to see a semi-transparent version of the other frames or an outline version. Click on the button for a second time to turn onion skinning off.

Onion Skinning | Modify Onion Markers
Outline Onion Skinning | Edit Multiple Frames

Onion Skinning Buttons at the Bottom of the Timeline

Onion Skinning

Outline Onion Skinning

19 When you have one of the onion skinning buttons selected, you will be able to drag out the onion skinning markers at the top of the Timeline and see more or less frames.

Onion Skinning Markers

20 If you are not happy with what you have done on a keyframe, you have two options:

- The first option is to clear the keyframe. Select the keyframe by clicking on it in the **Timeline**. You can then choose **Modify** > **Timeline** > **Clear Keyframe**. This will delete the changes that you made on that particular keyframe and you revert back to what was on the keyframe before. You will still have the same number of frames overall.

- The second option is to choose **Edit** > **Timeline** > **Remove Frames**. This has a similar effect, but your overall sequence will have one less frame, because the frame itself has been deleted rather than it contents cleared.

21 If you have a still image in your animation, for example a background that won't need to move, you only need to use one initial keyframe and then extend its duration with frames.

Select the Final Frame to Extend to

Insert Frames

22 In this case, select the final frame that you want to extend to and then **Insert** > **Timeline** > **Frame** or **F5**.

23 Play back your animation by using either the **playback controls** or press **ENTER** on your keyboard. If you can't see the **playback controls**, go to **Window** > **Toolbars** > **Controller**. Under the **Control** menu, you can select the **Loop Playback** option if you want to see your animation played back and repeated.

Don't forget to save regularly!

Frame Rate and Size

What is frame rate? This term refers to how many images you will be showing over time. It is measured in frames per second.

You can see the frame rate of your movie at the bottom of the Timeline measured in frames per second. Clicking on this figure acts as a shortcut to open the **Document Properties** dialog box.

If you have a high frame rate, like 25 or 30 frames per second, your animation will look smooth. If you have a low frame rate, like five frames per second, your animation will look jerky.

However, the accuracy of the playback depends on the speed of your CPU. Many computers cannot handle playing back your animation within Flash at 25 or 30 frames per second and will drop frames. If this is the case with your computer, you will need to export a small test movie to see your timing accurately. You could also try to lower the quality of your preview to ensure smoother playback by choosing **View** > **Preview Mode** > **Outlines** or **Fast**.

How do I know what frame rate to use? The more frames you have per second, the larger your file size will be. If you are animating for the web you most certainly do not want a high frame rate, because you want to keep your file sizes as small as possible. A standard frame rate for web animation would be somewhere between 10–15 frames per second. Experiment and choose the frame rate that works best for you.

How do I know what frame size to use? If you are creating animations for the web, you can choose the size of your movie according to the size that you want it to be on your web page. However, there is a fixed size if you want to put your animation onto video. See Chapter 12 *Video* for more information about this.

Can't I just change these settings after my animation is finished?

It is best practice to make sure you have the **correct frames per second** set up **before** you start, because it is not so easy to change once your animation is started.

For example, if you have done a 5 seconds animation at 15 frames per second with keyframes at 1second intervals and then you change the frame rate to 30 frames per second, Flash won't re-scale the time.

The **Timeline** measures time in **frames** not in **seconds** so your keyframes will still be at frames 15, 30, 45, 60, 75, but your animation will have been speeded up to last for 2½ seconds.

Test it out for yourself!

Similarly if you enlarge your **document** size after you have finished your animation, the whole animation will have moved to the top left-hand corner.

To move it back you can use the **Edit Multiple Frames** button in the Timeline.

Edit Multiple Frames Button

After you have selected this button, you will be able to see markers at the top of the Timeline. Drag them to cover all of the frames in your animation and then choose **Edit > Select All**.

Now drag your animation back to its original position. Don't forget to click the button a second time to deselect it.

Animation with Graphic Symbols

Animating frame-by-frame has its advantages, as long as you can draw in perspective, you can make characters spin around and move fluidly in different directions.

Sometimes it can be hard to visualize what an object or character would look like from different directions. If you are having problems with this, I would recommend making a little model of your character and using it for reference.

The disadvantage of frame-by-frame animation, however, is that there is lots of hard work drawing all of those pesky frames!

Luckily there is another way to animate in Flash in which the computer does much more of the work. You can create **graphic symbols**, which are re-usable drawings. Once you have created a symbol, you can alter it in successive keyframes, apply **motion tweening,** and Flash will draw all the frames in-between the keyframes.

Creating Graphic Symbols and Instances

1 Draw a character or shape to be animated and name the layer appropriately.

2 This kind of animation works best if each separate item to be animated is on a different layer. So, if your character has several moving parts, each one will need a separate layer. Name each layer so that you can remember what's on it.

3 As with the **button** and **movie clip** symbols that we created earlier, **graphic** symbols can be created in two ways:

- create your artwork on the Stage, make sure it is all selected and then choose **Modify > Convert to Symbol. Name it** and choose **graphic** behavior from the dialog box.

or

- select **Insert > New Symbol**. After naming your new symbol and choosing graphic as its behavior, you will be presented with an empty Stage on which to create your new symbol.

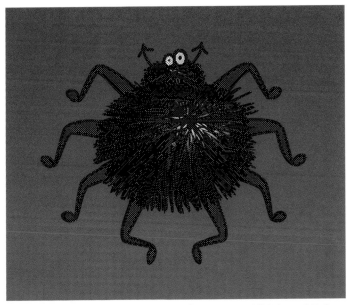

Create Artwork on the Stage and Make Sure it is All Selected Before You Convert it to a Symbol

4 You can give your graphic symbol any name that you feel like, however if you are working with programmers, they will be your friend if you prefix your graphic symbol names with **'g'**, for example **gSpider**.

5 Just as with the **button** and **movie clip** symbols that we looked at earlier, you can find your original symbols in the Library. Your **graphic** symbol can also be re-used many times in your scene, by dragging it from the **preview** window of this panel onto the Stage.

Your Original Symbol is in the Library. You Change Copies of it on the Stage

6 As we have seen in Chapters 6 and 7, the symbol that you see in the Library is the original version. The version of the symbol that you are using on the Stage is a copy of this original and is known as an **instance**.

7 Create a **keyframe** in frame 30 by clicking in the Timeline in frame 30 and selecting **Insert** > **Timeline** > **Keyframe** or **F6**.

8 This creates a copy of the previous keyframe, so you can see your **instance** in exactly the same position as it was in the last keyframe. You can now **move** the instance with the **Selection** tool and also **resize** or **rotate** it with the **Free Transform** tool.

Three Different Instances of the Same Symbol

9 You have other options as well. When you are on a keyframe and an **instance** is selected, you can see its property options in the Properties Inspector panel underneath the Stage. If you can't see it, choose **Window** > **Properties**.

Properties Inspector Panel

10 In the Properties Inspector panel you can select different values to change from the dropdown box next to **Color**.

- **Brightness** allows you to make your instance lighter or darker than the original symbol.

- **Tint** allows you to give the instance a different color than the original symbol.

- **Alpha** allows you to make the instance transparent. All three of these have a slider, which controls the amount of the effect.

- **Advanced** lets you use a combination of these.

11 So far you should have two different keyframes on your Timeline with an **instance** that has been altered on the second keyframe.

12 If you were to play back this project so far, there would not be any animation. The first version of the image would just instantly become the second on the last keyframe without any stages in between. In other words, there is no interpolation going on in-between these two keyframes.

Motion Tweening

Click on a Frame In-between Your Keyframes

Frame Properties

13 Now click somewhere on the frames in-between these two keyframes that you created earlier to select these frames. You will now be able to see the **Frame** properties in the Properties Inspector panel underneath your Stage.

14 In Flash, as in life, there are often many different ways to do the same thing and there are different ways to apply **motion tweening**. Once you know the different methods, you can choose the one that is easiest for you.

- Once you have selected the **in-between** frames in the middle of two keyframes, you can then choose **Insert** > **Timeline** > **Create Motion Tween**.

- Alternately, you can **CTRL/RIGHT-CLICK** on this point and select **Create Motion Tween** from the dropdown menu.

Choosing Motion from the Tween Options in the Properties Inspector

- Finally, if you have selected the **in-between** frames in the middle of two keyframes, you can then select **Motion** from the **Tween** drop-down box in the property inspector.

15 The in-between frames should now be pale blue and have an arrow pointing from one to the other.

A Successful Motion Tween

16 When you see this arrow, you know that your tween has been successful. If, however, you don't see an arrow and instead see a dotted line – something has gone wrong!

An Unsuccessful Motion Tween

17 The most common reasons that your tween may have gone wrong are:

- You forgot to use symbols – motion tweening doesn't work properly without converting your graphics to symbols,

- You have more than one symbol on your layer – again this doesn't work well,

or

- You converted your graphic retrospectively into a symbol and it changed in one of the keyframes but not in the other. The best way to deal with this is usually to select the second keyframe, choose **Edit > Timeline > Clear Keyframe** and start again.

18   Turning on **Onion Skinning** will allow you to see the in-between frames that Flash has created for you.

The first keyframes   The in-between frames   The last keyframes

A Motion Tween

19   Save and press **enter** to preview.

Graphic Symbols and Line Weights

Graphic symbols are useful for creating animation. They are also good to use if you have a static piece of artwork that you want to repeat with variations, for example clouds in a sky scene.

You may have noticed that if you create a piece of artwork using either **object or merge drawing** modes and re-scale it, the thickness of the stroke is not re-scaled. However, if you convert the same artwork into a **graphic symbol** and re-scale it, the line weight gets thinner as the shape gets smaller.

Editing Symbols Recap

Although you cannot seem to alter your symbol on the Stage, it is possible make changes to it.

To recap on Chapter 6, just as with **button** and **movie clip** symbols, if you go into your **Library** panel and select **Edit** from the **Options menu** at the top right-hand side, you enter into **Edit Symbol mode**. You will now be able to change your symbol and all the copies or **instances** on the Stage will change too.

Be careful, because it is quite easy to start editing your symbol without realizing that you are doing so. Here's why and what to do about it:

1   You should by now have got into the habit of double-clicking on a shape that you have drawn to select it, to make sure that both the stroke and fill are selected.

2   However, if you double-click on a symbol to select it, you will find that there is no longer a blue bounding box and that your symbol can now be altered. You may also wonder where the rest of your layers have gone and why the rest of your scene appears pale. The reason for this is that you have taken a shortcut for **Edit > Edit in Place**. This allows you to edit your symbol while still seeing the rest of the Stage.

3   As before, click on **Scene 1** on the information bar at the top left of the Stage to get back to your scene.

Summary

Over the years, I have found that some people find the concept of animating in Flash with symbols, keyframes and motion tweening to be complicated. If this is the case for you, just remember that if you can get to grips with it, you will save a lot of time and effort. It is also possible to combine this method of animation with the frame-by-frame method of animating.

So, here is a summary of the animation process in Flash:

1   **The simplest way to create animation in Flash is to draw each change that you want to happen on the Stage over time. This is just like creating traditional animation with a line tester.**

2   **With this method of *frame-by-frame animation* you need to create a new *keyframe* in the Timeline every time you want something different to happen on the Stage.**

A Frame-By-Frame Animation – Every Single Frame is Created Manually

3   If you want a drawing to *move, resize, rotate, change color* or *transparency* over time, you don't have to draw these changes on every frame: you can save time by creating a re-usable piece of graphic called a *graphic symbol* and alter it over time.

4   Each time you want this symbol to change, you will need to insert a new *keyframe* onto the Timeline. A *keyframe* is a frame on which a change is recorded.

5   Flash can create all the stages of change in-between your keyframes if you use symbols. In order to instruct the computer to create all these in-between frames between your keyframes, you will need to select those frames and create a *motion tween*.

The Frames In-between the Keyframes are Created Automatically

A Tweened Animation

6   Your original *symbol* can be accessed in the *Library*. What you are working with on the Stage are copies or *instances* of the original graphic symbol.

This Tween Doesn't Work Because there is More One Symbol on the Layer

7   You can use many copies of the same symbol on the Stage at the same time, but in order to *motion tween* them *individually* in *different ways* they will all need to be on *separate layers*.

8   Motion tweened animations have smaller file sizes than frame-by-frame animations. This is because you are making

133

alterations to a pre-defined symbol rather than starting a new piece of drawing from scratch on each frame and this information takes up less storage space on the computer.

9   Remember to make your symbol a *graphic symbol* for straightforward *animation*. The other types of symbols available are used for interactivity. *Movie clip* symbols *won't* play back on the Timeline properly.

CHAPTER 9

MORE ANIMATION TECHNIQUES

Using Motion Paths

A **motion path** is a drawing of the shape of the movement that you would like the symbol you are animating to take. You can draw these on **guide layers** in Flash. **Guide layers** can also be used to add lines and shapes that you are only using for layout and reference purposes. When you render your final movie, you won't see anything that has been created on a **guide layer**:

1 Draw a shape that you would like to animate and turn it into a **graphic symbol**. Make sure that it is on it's own layer. Create a second **keyframe** in frame 30 and create some **motion tweening** between these two frames. You need to do this so that you have more than one keyframe to place on your motion path.

Add motion   Guide layer   The 'guided' layer
guide icon   is indented

Two Motion Tweened Keyframes

2 Now to create a motion path. Make sure the layer you want to effect is selected. Select **Insert > Timeline > Motion Guide** or more simply click on the **Add Motion Guide** icon at the bottom of the timeline. This will create a new layer called **Guide: (*name of layer effected*)**. The layer underneath, which will be effected by the motion guide, should be indented.

3 A guide layer won't show up in your final movie. You could also use it to write little notes and reminders to yourself or your co-workers while you are working.

Motion Guide that we Want to be the Flight Path of the Bird

4 Click on the guide layer's name to make it active. Select the **Pencil** tool and the **Smooth** modifier. Draw a curved path on frame 1. If it is not smooth enough, click on the **Selection** tool and then double click on the path to select it all. Next click on the **Selection** tool **Smooth** modifier again and again until you achieve the desired result. You can draw a **motion path** with the **pencil** or **pen** tools.

5 Your motion guide layer should have been automatically extended to a length of 30 frames, because this is the length of the motion tween you created. If for some reason it hasn't, insert blank frames to extend it, by selecting the frames up to frame 30 and then **Insert** > **Timeline** > **Frame** or **F5**.

Snap is turned on in the Toolbox

Smooth modifier

6 Make sure **snap** is **turned on** in the **Toolbox** as well as in the **Properties** window. Then, checking that you are in frame 1, drag your character/ shape by its center point until it snaps to the starting point of the path you just drew.

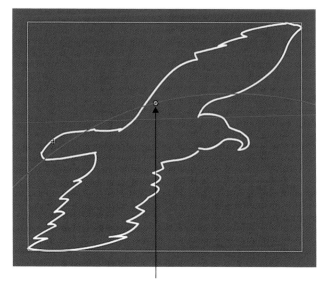

The center point of the bird symbol
snapping to the start of the motion path

7   Go to frame 30 and drag to the end of the motion path as above.
Check that in frames 5 and 25 your object is also snapping to your
path.

Click here to hide the
visibility of a layer

8   Once everything is working for you, click in the eye icon column to select
Hidden for the Motion Path layer.

9   Save and press **ENTER** to preview.

10   In order to change the symbol's orientation as it progresses along the
path, access the **Properties** window for frames by clicking in between

**The Visibility of the Guide Layer is Turned Off, but Onion Skinning
Shows that the Bird Symbol is Now Following the Motion Path**

Orient to path   Snap   Expansion triangle

Add number of rotations here
to make the symbol spin

Frame Properties Inspector

two keyframes on the timeline. The Properties Inspector will now show
you the **Frame Properties** with different options for tweening.

11   Now select **Orient to path**. You might need to expand your **Properties**
window in order to see this option. You can do this by clicking on the
small downward pointing expansion triangle in the bottom right-hand
corner of this panel.

12   You could also opt to have your symbol rotating by selecting
Rotate > CW (Clockwise) or **(CCW) Counter Clockwise** and specifying
the number of rotations.

The Same Bird Example with Onion Skin Outline and Orient to Path Applied

Controlling Velocity

1 When you **motion tween** between two keyframes, the changes that take place happen at a constant speed. In the real physical world, however, changes don't take place at a constant speed. If you were to kick a football, the initial force of the kick would mean that the ball would start off moving fast and then as friction, gravity,

Easing in the Properties Inspector

etc. acted on it, it would start to slow down. Flash can enable you to add a certain amount of acceleration and deceleration to tweens. This is done through **easing**.

2 Click in between two keyframes on the timeline and then look at your **Frame Properties** window. One of the options is called **easing**. This controls the amount of acceleration or deceleration in the changes between two keyframes. If you drag the slider down to get a negative number – this adds acceleration. Moving the slider up to get a positive number adds deceleration.

Custom Easing

If you have bought the Professional version of Flash, you will have the option to customize the easing through the use of a graph.

Click on the **Ease Edit** button in the **Frame Properties** window.

Choose the property to apply easing to

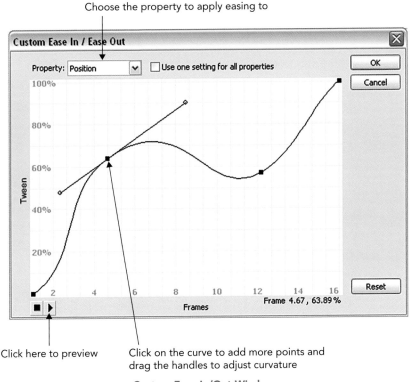

Click here to preview   Click on the curve to add more points and
                               drag the handles to adjust curvature

Custom Ease In/Out Window

Shape Tweening

So far we have looked at animating symbols with **motion tweening** so that the software creates the 'inbetweens' for you. Flash can also transform one drawing

141

or graphic shape into another and create the '*inbetweens*' that describe the changes from the first drawing to the second. This process is called **shape tweening**.

You **do not use symbols** when you are shape tweening. You use plain artwork created in either **object** or **merge drawing** mode.

First off, the basics:

1 Start a new file. Draw a circle on frame 1. Insert a **blank** keyframe into frame 30.

2 Turn on **onion skinning** so that you can see where the circle you just drew was positioned.

3 Select the **rectangle tool**. Change the **fill color, stroke color** and **line style** and draw a rectangle roughly over the position of the circle. Turn **off** onion skinning.

4 On the **timeline**, click on the frames that are in between the 2 keyframes you just created so that you can see the **Frame Properties** window. Select **Shape** from the **Tween** menu.

Draw a Rectangle in One Keyframe and a Circle in Another. Use Onion Skinning to Align their Positions

Frame Properties Window

5 Note that in the **Properties** window you can apply **easing** to a shape tween just as you can to a motion tween. This will allow you to have more of the starting or ending shape shown. **Blend** refers to how the morphing will be applied: **distributive** emphasizes **curves** and **angular** emphasizes **angles**.

▼ Timeline

👁 🔒 ☐ 1   5   10   ▌15   20   25   3

🗁 shape tween ⬗ • • ☐ |•⟩——————————————————⟩|•

A Successful Shape Tween

6 The frames that you clicked in on the Timeline should now be green and there should be an arrow from keyframe to keyframe. This indicates that your tween has worked with no problems.

▼ Timeline

👁 🔒 ☐ 1   5   10   15   20   25   3

🗁 shape tween ⬗ • • ☐ |•••|

An Unsuccessful Shape Tween

7 If you have a dotted line between the two keyframes, this indicates that something has gone wrong with your tween. The most common

First frame   Inbetween frames   Last frame
                      created by shape tween
Expanded View of the Shape Tween

reasons are that you tried to shape tween (a) a symbol, (b) a group or (c) editable text (more on how to shape tween text next). None of these will work.

8 Press **ENTER** to preview.

Shape Tweening Text

Now let's look at shape tweening text and how to control a shape tween. This doesn't work with standard editable text. You have to break the text apart first. As the software is creating the '*inbetweens*' for you, the results may be unpredictable. However, you do have a certain amount of control over this process through the use of **easing**, **blend type** and **shape hints**:

1 Type your name onto a new layer with a size of 72 points.

2 **Insert** a **keyframe** into all the layers on frame 30. Change the font that is used on this keyframe.

Breaking Apart Text

3 Shape tweening doesn't work for standard text so you have to turn them into editable vectors by selecting them and then **Modify > Break Apart** or **⌘/CTRL + B**. You have to do this twice and the second time you are changing the letters from editable text into a vector graphic.

The First Time You Select *Break apart* You are Ungrouping the Letters

The Second Time You Select Break Apart the Letters Become Graphic Objects

4 Make sure that the text is also broken apart twice in frame 30. Select the frames between the keyframes and select **shape** for the **tweening** type from the **frame panel**.

5 Save and press **ENTER** to preview.

The Result May Look Quite Strange in the Middle

Controlling Shape Tweens with Shape Hints

6 Flash may need more information about which points in the letters correspond to the same points in the second style of letters. **Shape hints** can rectify the tween.

Adding Shape Hints

145

7   Look at the animation carefully and work out in which places Flash becomes confused. In frame 1 select the required letter and **Modify > Shape > Add Shape Hint**. You may have to zoom out to find it and then zoom in again to place it accurately.

8   Go to frame 30 and move the shape hint to the corresponding place on the letter.

9   Keep saving, previewing and adding more shape hints until you achieve a smooth morph from one letter to another. Unfortunately, sometimes shape hints don't untangle your shape, so don't be disappointed if it doesn't work as expected.

Expanded Text Shape Tween

Shape Tweening Summary

Note. *Shape tweening* is an entirely different process to *motion tweening*.

Motion tweening refers to an *original symbol*. The copies or *instances* that you are working with have a relationship with the original.

On the other hand, *shape tweening* is the process whereby one image turns into another entirely *unrelated* image. To create a shape tween, therefore, you *do not use symbols*, because you are not simply modifying an original but morphing it into something totally *new*.

Shape tweening can be useful for animating gradients and for changing one facial expression into another. This technique can also be used to transform one traced bitmap into another with very interesting results. However, be warned that this will be very slow for your computer to process.

Create Animated Text Highlights

Creating masks allows you to mask out areas of the screen. When you create a mask layer it hides part of the layer underneath. Your mask can be animated. You could use a mask layer to give the impression of looking through a keyhole or through a pair of binoculars. Beware though, spotlight effects are seen by some as a Flash cliché.

In this example, we will create an animated gradient and then put a mask in the shape of a word over it. This will give the impression that light is moving across the text:

1   Firstly, create the text that the effect will show through.

Create Some Bold Text

2   Select the **text tool**, click somewhere on the stage, and type **<FLASH>** or another word of your choice. Use a big, bold, chunky font so that the text looks dramatic and clearly seen. Don't spend time trying to perfect the color of your text, as it will be used as a **mask** later, and you won't be able to see its color.

3   This should be the top layer as it will be masking the layer underneath. Name this layer **<text mask>**.

4   Next to create the effect which will be showing through your text. **Insert**
a **new layer**. Drag this new layer underneath the layer you just created
the mask on. Name this new layer **<gradient>**.

The Layers

Animating and Transforming Gradients

5   Select the **Rectangle tool**, make sure that there will be no outline on it
by clicking in the **Stroke Color Control** and clicking the white box with a
red line through it. Draw the rectangle so that it stretches off screen.
Then click the rectangle you just made and open the **Color Mixer panel**.
If you can't see it, choose **Window > Color Mixer**.

Create a Narrow Gradient for the Rectangle

6   Select **Linear** from the **Fill Style** dropdown menu. Make a linear
gradient that goes from gray to white to gray, dragging in the two
outer tabs to make the white portion narrow compared to the rest of
the gradient.

7 First making sure now that your rectangle is *not* selected, choose the **Transform Fill tool** to **rotate** the 'glint' to a 45° angle. You might need to choose a magnification of 50% or even 25% in order to see the **Transform Fill handles**, which you use to rotate and re-scale fills with.

Rotate the gradient to an angle with the transform fill tool by dragging on this handle

Drag the Gradient Fill to the Left

8 Next drag the gradient fill all the way to the left so that the central white stripe is at the back to the left-hand side of the text.

9 We want to make it look as if the effect is moving across the text, which will stay stationary. Make a keyframe on the gradient layer at frame 30 and use the **Transform Fill tool** again to drag the gradient over to the right-hand side. Next choose *shape* **tween** from the **Properties Inspector** so that the gradient moves from one side of the stage to the other.

Drag the Gradient Fill to the Right

10 Select frame 30 of the text layer and **insert frame** so that the text layer exists for the same amount of frames as the rectangle. This will make sure that the text stays on the stage while the effect rolls along.

Mask Layers

11 Make sure your **gradient** layer is **beneath** your **mask** layer. Making sure that the **mask** layer is the active layer **CTRL/RIGHT-CLICK** on the **text layer** and choose **Mask** from the pop up. Your text should now be filled by the rectangle that you made.

12 Press **ENTER** to preview – the highlight should travel across the text.

Choose Mask from the Menu

The Layers with Masking Applied

The Highlight Travels Across the Text

13 Both layers are now locked. If you want to remove the masking, unlock the layer and **CTRL/RIGHT-CLICK** on the **text layer** and choose **Mask** from the pop up a second time.

14 Be creative and experiment with this basic idea – for example import a bitmap and animate it moving behind some text, fade the 'gleam' in and out, create an animation, which shows through some text.

15 You can soften the edge of the mask with the use of gradients. The mask itself can also be animated. Horizontal stripes and circles can be used as masks to give the effect of film transitions. Finally, masks can apply to more than one layer if these layers are indented underneath it.

CHAPTER 10

FURTHER ANIMATION TECHNIQUES

Timeline Effects

Timeline Effects are prebuilt effects allowing you to easily create and duplicate animated **text, graphic symbols, shapes** and **groups**, imported **bitmaps, button and movie clip symbols**:

 To apply a **Timeline Effect**, select the object you want to apply it to and then select the required Effect from the **Insert** menu.

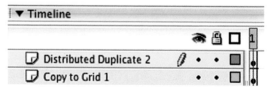

The Copy to Grid Effect, which Creates a Grid Out of the Shape You've Selected

2 **Insert** > **Timeline Effects** > **Assistants** > **Copy to Grid** creates copies in the shape of a grid.

3 **Update Preview** allows you to see the changes that you have made to the Effect parameters.

Layers are Named after the Effect Applied

4 The settings are saved within a graphic symbol that can be found in your library with the rest of your symbols and imported bitmaps.

5 If you want to separate the grid into individual pieces, then choose **Modify** > **Break Apart**.

6 **Insert** > **Timeline Effects** > **Assistants** > **Distributed Duplicate** creates copies in a line, which can be rotated and have different colors applied.

The New Graphic Symbols are also named after the Effect

Distributed Duplicate applied to a Star Shape

7 **Insert** > **Timeline Effects** > **Effects** > **Blur** is used to create an animated fade out.

8 Insert > Timeline Effects > Effects > Drop Shadow allows you to create a drop shadow. Entering positive numbers into the **Shadow Offset** boxes will place your shadow in the bottom left corner. Entering negative numbers in both the **X** and **Y** boxes will place your shadow in the top right corner. Unfortunately, there is no control to allow you to rotate or skew the drop shadow, so I prefer to create them manually as per the example in Chapter 6.

First Frame of an Expanded Text Sequence

9 Insert > Timeline Effects > Effects > Expand. This Effect creates an animated rescaling. As with **Explode**, it is most successful when used with text.

10 Insert > Timeline Effects > Effects > Explode. This Effect gives the illusion of an explosion with pieces rotating away from the center.

11 **Transform** allows you to animate position, rotation, scale and transparency all in one go. This can be found by accessing **Insert > Timeline Effects > Transform/Transition > Transform**.

Four Stages of a Wipe Transition

12   **Transition** allows you to add a fade or wipe transition.

13   To edit your **Timeline Effect** after it has been applied, choose **Modify > Timeline Effect > Edit**.

14   To remove your **Timeline Effect**, choose **Modify > Timeline Effect > Remove Effect**.

Animated Symbols

When you create a **graphic symbol**, you may have noticed that it contains layers and a timeline of its own, just like with the **button** and **movie clip symbols** we looked at earlier. You can use this to create an animated symbol. **Why would you want to do that?**

Expanded Version of an Animated Graphic Symbol Containing a Frame-by-Frame Animation of a Bird in Flight

1   In this example I have created a new graphic symbol. It contains a frame-by-frame animation of a bird in flight.

The Frames within the Symbol

157

2   The flying eagle animation lasts for 16 frames.

▼ Timeline

| | | | | | 1 | 5 | 10 | 15 | 20 | 25 | 30 | 35 |

🗒 flying eagle

The Flying Eagle Layer lasts for 32 Frames.
Therefore, the Animation will Loop Twice

3   When placed on the timeline the flying eagle animated symbol will loop after 16 frames. In order to see the animated loop, you will need to insert some frames onto the timeline. If you insert 16 frames it will play once. With 32 frames it will play twice and with 160 it will play 10 times, etc.

4   Just like a static graphic symbol, the **animated graphic symbol** can be made to follow a **motion path**. You can also apply all of the other types of animated changes that work with motion

The Animated Graphic Symbol following a Motion Path

tweening. Your animated symbol can also **move, resize, rotate, change color** or **transparency** and be **motion tweened**.

5   In other words, you can use animated graphic symbols to **animate pieces or cycles of animation** with **motion tweening**. This is a great way

Onion Skin Outlines shows how the Animated
Symbol is following the Motion Path

to use animated cycles, such as the up and down flap of a bird's wing in this example. When a cycle is repeated it gives the impression of continuous movement. So in this example, the bird can be made to fly across the screen, following a curved motion path and changing in scale to give the impression of distance.

6 When you use animated graphic symbols, you can choose which frame you want the looped piece of animation to start on. This is done in the **Properties** window.

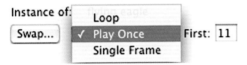

Options for Graphic Symbols in the Properties Inspector

7 Click on your animated graphic symbol to select it and from the **options for graphics** in the **Properties** window you will be able to choose whether you want your piece of animation to **loop, play once** or just show a **single frame**. You can also add a number into the **First:** box, which specifies the first frame that will be shown.

8 This means that you can have several copies of the same piece of animation all playing at the same time, but all starting on a different frame. Very handy for a flock of birds!

**A Flock of Birds Created by Starting the same Animated
Graphic Symbol Loops on Different Frames**

Creating a Looped Background

Another use for animated graphic symbols is to create a looped background. For example, if you had a character walking on the spot, you might want to have a looped background of scenery going past in the background – adding to the illusion of the character walking through space.

A tip for creating a perfect loop is to start by making your first frame exactly the same as your last frame. Create the scenery moving and then returning to the last frame.

If you used the loop like this, there would be a slight jump as the first and last frames are the same. So create keyframes on the second last frame and then delete the last frame.

Your loop should now play endlessly without you being able to see the join.

Copying and Pasting Frames

At times you may create a complicated animation on the Stage and wish that you had created it all within one animated symbol. Perhaps you want to animate the scale of the whole scene so that it looks as if you are zooming in with a camera. Perhaps you would like to use an animated circular mask on the whole scene to give the impression of an iris wipe transition.

It is possible to take animation from the Stage and convert it all into one animated graphic symbol, which you can then motion tween as a whole. Here's how:

1 Click on the name of the first layer you want to select. Clicking on the layer name selects all of the keyframes and frames on that layer.

Four Layers and all Their Frames are Selected

2   Then hold down the **SHIFT** key and click on the names of all the other layers that you want to select. By now all the frames and keyframes on all of the layers you want will be selected.

3   Next choose **Edit > Timeline > Copy Frames – ⌘/CTRL + ALT + C** (or if you are feeling brave **Edit > Timeline > Cut Frames – ⌘/CTRL + ALT + X**).

4   Then create a new graphic symbol – **Insert > New Symbol**.

5   Click into frame 1 of layer 1 in your new symbol and then **Edit > Timeline > Paste Frames – ⌘/CTRL + ALT + V**. All your layers and frames will now have been pasted into the new symbol and your layers will even retain the names you gave them.

6   This new animated graphic symbol containing all of your animation will be in the **Library**. Go back to your main scene, delete the original layers you copied, make a new, fresh layer and then drag in the new animated symbol that you created.

7   Add frames so that the new symbol lasts on the timeline for the same duration as the previous animation. You do not need to use keyframes.

Symbols Within Symbols

Just as you can animate a graphic symbol using its own timeline and layers, so you also bring other graphic symbols into a graphic symbol. Here is an example of a whole character built with graphic symbols that are contained within one whole graphic symbol:

1   This figure is jointed like a puppet. It uses very few basic symbols.

The Various Symbols Making up the whole Character, Which is itself a Symbol

The ankle, knee, shoulder, elbow, hip joints and waist are all made from the same basic graphic symbol. All the parts of the limbs also use the same graphic symbol.

2 The character has been separated into different symbols according to how it will move and each of these symbols is on a separate layer so that they can be animated individually.

3 The individual symbols have been nested together in a hierarchy of symbols all contained within one symbol. The whole character has been created within one symbol so that it can be motion tweened as a whole.

4 If you group elements of the body together in sections, then you can manipulate these whole sections together as one piece and still have the option to move the individual symbols. However, grouping elements together that are on **different layers** through **Modify > Group** is **not** very successful in Flash.

5 A more effective way to achieve this is by grouping elements together by placing several body parts into a new combined graphic symbol. This is done by selecting symbols on the stage and **Modify > Convert to Symbol**.

6 So for example, you could select the **foot** and the **calf** symbols and convert them into a new composite graphic symbol called **lower leg**.

7 The following flow charts show how the graphic symbols making up the **leg** and **arm** were built into a hierarchy in this example.

The Arm and Leg Symbols

8 So even though the leg contains several parts, all of these parts can be moved together as one.

Altering Symbol Center Points

9 Our skeletal structure works by rotation – our body parts rotate around our joints, so we need to make sure that each element that we want to animate can also be rotated around the correct joints.

Changing the Center of Rotation for the Leg and Arm Symbols

10 Each of the **leg** and **arm** composite symbols has its center point changed to the center of the nearest joint. This was done with the **Free Transform** tool. So the center point of the leg symbol has been moved to the hip point and the center point of the arm has been moved to the shoulder.

11 Now if the **leg** is rotated and it will move around the **hip joint** and the **arm** will rotate around the **shoulder joint**.

163

12 If you double click on the **leg** symbol, you will now have access to the **thigh** and **lower leg symbols**. The center point of the **lower leg symbol** was changed to the **knee joint** with the **Free Transform** tool.

Changing the Center of Rotation to the Knee and the Elbow

13 Each time you double click on a symbol, you go one level deeper into the hierarchy that you have made and you can make adjustments. Your character can now be manipulated like a jointed puppet.

Using Scenes

Each Flash project that you work on can be divided into **Scenes**. This can be very useful if you are working on a story and you want the freedom to easily be able to reorder the different sequences.

The **Scene panel** can be accessed from the **Window** menu under **Other panels**.

Just like layers, **Scenes** can be dragged up and down to change their order. Scenes at the top of the list are shown first and those at the bottom are shown last.

To rename a Scene, double click on its name.

Scene Panel

Character Design Tips

What kind of personality does your character have? How it moves will give a lot of clues about your character. Think about the joints and the mechanics of the movement – where does a figure bend, how do the pieces fit together and how do they move?

Create model sheets for your characters showing them from the side, front and three quarters views and with different expressions.

Use this as the starting point for a library of parts for your character – mouth shapes, costume changes, hairstyles, etc.

It can be hard to imagine what your character might look like in motion or from different angles so:

- buy toys or models of a similar shape,

- sculpt plasticine or clay models,

- use mirrors to look at yourself from different angles,

- video your friends,

- make quick sketches of passers by out in public.

CHAPTER 11
SOUND

Creating Sounds to Bring into Flash

There are lots of places on the web to download free sound files – legally! The accompanying website contains links to some such sites. If you are a music whiz kid, on the other hand, you may want to compose your own soundtracks using software such as Adobe Audition or Cubase.

You cannot import a music track into Flash from an audio CD. It is not in the correct format to be used in Flash and if you do not have permission this would be infringing copyright.

It can be fun to record your own sounds. These could be **foley effects** – sound effects you make yourself – such as banging two halves of a coconut together to make the sound of horses hooves – or **voice** recording.

Capturing sound on a Mac or a PC depends on your computer having a soundcard installed. Most recent machines should have one.

Sound Recording
Utility on a PC

On a PC there are different brands of soundcard and each one has its own generic sound program. The Windows operating system also comes with a **Sound Recorder**, which you should be able to find somewhere in **Start > Programs > Accessories > Entertainment**. When you have located a sound capture program, all that remains is to plug a microphone into your soundcard and sing your heart out! Remember to make sure that the levels indicator doesn't go into the red.

On a Mac, if you don't have a specialized sound program, you can use **iMovie** to record sounds and then **export** them as audio only QuickTime movies.

The sound tools in Flash are quite limited, so it is best to create the sound file exactly as you want to use it in your audio software before you bring it into Flash.

In order to bring sounds into Flash, they must have been saved as one of the following sound file formats:

- **WAV** (Windows only)

- **AIFF** (Mac only)

- **MP3** (both)

If you have QuickTime 4 or later loaded onto your computer, you will also be able to use **WAV**s on a Mac, **AIFF**s on a PC and audio only **QuickTime** movies. See the Flash Help files for information on more specialized sound formats.

MP3s are a good file format to use because they effectively compress sound providing good quality at lower file sizes.

Some Fundamentals of Digital Audio

WAVs, **AIFF**s, **MP3**s and audio only **QuickTime** movies are complete representations of the sound information. They are a bit like **bitmaps**.

MIDI (musical instrument digital interface) files are also used by musicians to transmit sound information. They are not, however, a complete representation of a sound, but a series of mathematical note instructions – a bit like a **vector**. Flash cannot read these files – they need a sequencer to be played back.

When you record a sound on your computer you are actually converting a natural sound vibration in the shape of a wave into digital information. This is done by taking samples of the wave at regular intervals.

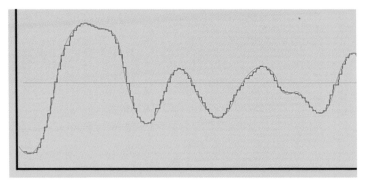

A Sound Sample. The Curved Blue Line shows the Shape of the Natural Sound Vibration. The Stepped Gray Line is the Digital Version of the Sound with Samples taken at Regular Intervals

The **frequency** of samples per second taken is measured in **kiloHertz**. The higher this number is the better the quality of the sound will be. You should be able to choose one of these rates in all sound editing programs:

5 kiloHertz   Roughly the quality of a phone call.

11 kiloHertz   Average TV quality (without Nicam stereo and surround sound).

22 kiloHertz   FM radio station with good reception.

44 kiloHertz   CD-ROM quality.

The other variable with sound recording is the **bit rate**. This is the amount of storage space given to each of the samples. Try to use as high a bit rate as your target file size will allow for, as this setting has a dramatic effect on sound quality.

Importing Sounds

To import a sound:

1   Choose **File > Import > Import to Library** and select the file you want to import.

Drag from here onto the Stage →

A Mono Sound File in the Library

Click here to hear the sound

A Stereo Sound File in the Library

2 Your sound file will now be stored in the Library along with any symbols you have created or bitmaps you have imported. Notice the **play** button in the Library thumbnail preview window.

3 Once you have some sound files in your Library, you can add them to your movie in two different ways:

- Just as you would with a bitmap or symbol, make a new layer for the sound to go on and then drag the sound file from the **Library** thumbnail preview window onto the **Stage**.

Choosing a Sound File from the Properties Inspector Window

- The other method is to click the first frame of a new sound layer and then select your chosen sound from the dropdown box next to **Sound:** in the **Properties** window.

4 It is best practice to make sure that each sound that you use is on its own individual layer.

5 Next you need to add frames for the whole duration of the sound. How do you know how many frames to add?

Sound Information in the Properties Inspector Window (Circled)

6 When the first frame of the sound layer is clicked on, information about the sound file is shown in the **Properties** window. This information shows the quality, length and file size of your sound. In the example above, the sound file is 7.2 seconds long.

7   Information about your sound file can also be accessed through the **Library**. Select the file by clicking on its name then choose **CTRL/ RIGHT-CLICK** or **Library** > **Options** > **Properties**.

8   To find out how many frames to add to your sound to be able to hear it all, use the following formula:

LENGTH OF SOUND × FRAME RATE

9   So in this example, if my project's frame rate is 25 frames per second, and the sound file is 7.2 seconds long – 7.2 × 25 = 180 – so I will need 180 frames in order to be able to hear all of the sound.

Audio Layers on the Timeline

10   Once you have all of the frames you need on the Timeline, you will be able to see the shape of the audio waveform.

Streaming vs. Event Sounds

The sound information in the Properties window, that you see whenever you have clicked on a frame of a sound layer, also contains an option called **Sync**. Select the type of audio sync that you require for your project.

The **Sync** option that you choose depends on what you want to do with a sound. There are four options:

1   **Stream** is used for animation and straightforward playback from the Timeline.

Audio Sync Options
in the Properties
Inspector

If **Stream** is selected, the sound will be 'scrubable' in other words, you can drag the playhead and hear a rough preview.

A **streaming** sound is synched to the Timeline – in other words, it will only last for the amount of frames that you have given it and will play along with any animation. If your animation is on the web and cannot be played back at full quality, the animation will drop frames to stay in synch with the audio.

Streaming sounds can start playing before they are completely downloaded.

2   **Event** sounds are played independently to the Timeline (in the same way that a Movie Clip symbol is independent of the Timeline). They need to be **triggered** by an **Event**, for example a **Button**.

Event sounds must be downloaded completely before they will play back. They must be explicitly stopped by a **Button**, **Behavior** or **Action**, or they will play right to the bitter end.

If the **event** is triggered several times, for example if a user pushes a button repeatedly, several instances of the sound will play at the same time.

3   **Start** is similar to **Event**, but will only play one instance of a sound if the event is triggered several times.

4   **Stop** will stop the sound playing. Use **Stop** on a new keyframe in your sound layer to make the sound stop.

As well as choosing what you want to use the sound for, you can also choose how many times you want it to play back in the Properties window.

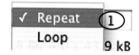

Repeating or Looping Sounds In the Properties Window

Choose **Repeat** and add a number in the box to determine how many times the sound will be repeated.

Choosing **Loop** will loop the sound endlessly.

Do not use **Loop** for **streaming** sounds with web animation, because it will add to the overall file size. It is preferable to specify exactly how many times you want the piece of audio to be repeated.

Editing Sounds in Flash

Flash is not a sound editing program, but there are a limited amount of effects and editing that can be applied to sounds.

The following **Effects** can be added to a sound from the Properties Inspector. When an effect is selected, you can click on **Edit** to see more information about it and to customize it:

Sound Effects in the Properties Inspector

- **None** – this is used to remove an effect that was previously applied.

- **Left Channel/Right Channel** – plays the sound only in that channel.

The Fade Right-to-Left Effect

- **Fade Left to Right/Fade Right to Left** – creates a 'panning' effect by shifting the sound from one channel to another.

- **Fade In/Fade Out** – the sound starts off quiet before increasing to full volume or the reverse.

- **Custom** – use this to create your own effect. It will open the **Edit** window.

Drag these to trim the 'in' and 'out' points of the sound

Click on this line to add a handle

Drag the handles up and down to change the levels

Effect: Custom

OK

Cancel

Edit Envelope

To preview the sound

Click here to see more or less of the sound file

To measure in frames

To measure in seconds

The Edit Window

Attach a Sound to a Button

1 Import the required files into your Library.

2 Create a button as before: **Insert > New Symbol > Button**.

3 Make a new layer called **sound** and **insert blank keyframes** in the **Up** and **Over** states.

4 If you want your button to make a sound when the cursor is over it, **insert** a **keyframe** in the **Over** frame.

5   Select this keyframe and choose the sound file you want to use from the **Sound:** dropdown list in the Properties Inspector.

6   Choose **Start** as your **Sync** type.

This Button will make a Sound When it is Clicked on

7   If you want your button to make a sound when it is clicked on, **insert** a **keyframe** in the **Down** frame and repeat stages 5 and 6 above.

8   Go back to your main scene and drag a copy of this button onto the Stage. Turn on **Control** > **Enable Simple Buttons** and drive your neighbors crazy by testing it out.

Starting and Stopping Sounds

An **event** sound can start or stop because this event has been triggered by a button. If you want to create a button that starts or stops a sound playing, you can do this using **behaviors**. The **Behaviors** panel contains scripts such as '**Play Sound**', '**Stop Sound**' or '**Stop all Sounds**', which you can attach to buttons just as we did in Chapter 7.

A **streaming** sound can be made to start or stop by creating keyframes on the sound layer and then selecting **Properties** > **Audio Sync** > **Stream** to start the sound and **Properties** > **Audio Sync** > **Stop** to stop the sound.

Adding Comments to Frames

If you are working with voice tracks, it can be useful to add comments as you are going along to remind you of what is said.

This can be especially valuable if you are animating a character's mouth shapes and facial expressions to match a piece of dialog. The **lip-synching** process depends on breaking speech down into sounds. Here's how to comment your voiceover:

1   Create a layer for your frame comments. **Insert** a **blank keyframe** where you want the first comment to be. Select this keyframe.

2   Type the letters of the sound into the Properties Inspector.

Add a Frame Label in the
Properties Inspector

Choose Comment as the
Label Type

3   Choose **Type** > **Comment**. This ensures that these comments will not be exported with your final movie and will keep your file size down.

The Speech is Broken Down into Sounds

Warning about File Sizes

Sound files can add enormously to the size of your project. If you are creating work for the Internet you will need to get those audio files as small as possible.

Tips for lowering audio file sizes:

1 Set in and out points that exclude silent areas.

2 Loop small pieces of sound for background music.

3 Try to use the same sound with different effects.

4 Stereo files are twice the size of mono files – do you really need stereo?

5 Repeat streaming sounds rather than looping them.

Chapter 14, **Putting Flash on the Web**, includes information about compressing audio and exporting movies with audio files.

CHAPTER 12

Digitizing Video

You cannot use Flash to take video directly from a tape or a camera. You will need to use a video-editing program like Adobe Premiere Pro, iMovie or Final Cut Pro for this.

In order to bring video into your computer, it must first be converted into a digital form that your computer will understand.
There are several ways to do this:

1 Use a **digital** video camera and input/output the video via an **IEEE 1394/Firewire cable** connected from the camera to an **IEEE 1394/Firewire port** on the computer.

2 Use a traditional **analogue** camera or video deck and connect this to a **video capture card** installed inside your computer. This will convert the information from analogue to digital.

3 Create moving images **in the computer** with an animation program.

Choosing Cameras at IBC, Amsterdam, Using Video in Flash

Using Video in Flash

Video can be imported as:

- **Macromedia Flash Video (FLV)**

Flash will also allow you to import the following moving image file formats if you are on a Mac or PC with QuickTime 7 or later installed:

- **AVI**
- **MPEG** (will not import audio on a Mac)
- **QuickTime**

If you are on a PC and have DirectX 9 or later installed, you can also import the following formats:

- **AVI**
- **MPEG**
- **Windows Media**

Video files are imported using either **Sorenson Spark compression** or **On2** depending on whether you intend to publish to Flash Player 7 or 8. These highly effective types of compression or **CODEC** enable video clips, which would normally have huge file sizes, to be embedded in or linked to Flash movies with impressive reductions in file sizes.

Start off with the highest quality video that you could possibly get. However, if you want to put your video on a web page then you must be prepared to compromise on its size. Here are some sample video frame sizes for different types of Internet connections:

Modem	**160 × 120**
Dual ISDN	**192 × 144**
T1/DSL/Cable	**320 × 240**

Creating FLV Files

If you have the professional version of Flash, you will be able to take advantage of more video features than if you have the basic version. This includes the Flash

Video Encoder, which is a stand-alone application allowing you to convert video files into the FLV format. It enables you to choose from various settings and to batch process several files at once.

Video Encoder (Pro Version). The Video Clips Used in this Chapter are all Come from a Pop Video for the Camarillos

The process of converting files is straightforward. **Add** the video files that you wish to convert. Choose the **settings** that you want to use and then **start queue** to process all your files.

If you have the professional version of Flash and QuickTime 6.1.1 or later, you can also export FLV files from the following supported video programs:

- **After Effects**

- **Final Cut Pro**

- **QuickTime Pro**

- **Avid Xpress DV**

Importing Video

To import video, follow these steps:

1   Make sure you have a new layer for the video to go on and then choose **File > Import > Import Video**. A Video Import 'wizard' will open to guide you through the import process. Select your video file.

2   Your first choice is how your video will be **deployed** in your final product. If you have a basic web site and not a streaming server, choose **Progressive download from a web server**. The playback will be a higher quality with a streaming server, but a standard web server should give you acceptable results.

Encoding your Video

3   The next stage of the wizard will prompt you to choose your encoding options. If you want to try to encode for a domestic modem, choose **Flash 7- Modem Quality (40 kbps)**. If you want to encode for broadband viewers choose one of the higher figures. If you have the professional version of Flash you will be able to customize these settings.

4   If you have the professional version, you will also be able to choose a 'skin', which determines the color and position of your playback controls. Your movie will be placed on the timeline as an **FLVPlayback component**. Select **Control > TestMovie** to see you video in action.

5 Do you want to embed a small video clip within an animation? This will greatly add to your file size, but can look good! Just be careful to use short clips. If so, in the **deployment** options choose **Embed video in SWF and play in timeline**. Then select your required encoding and embedding options. Flash will automatically add the number of frames needed to insert all of your video onto the Timeline.

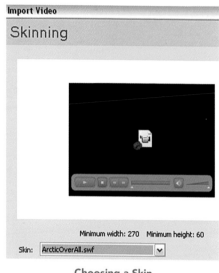

Choosing a Skin

6 Now the embedded video is imported and it can be manipulated like any other object – resized, rotated, skewed, moved and masked.

7 It can be used as a background layer with graphics and drawings on the layers above.

FLVPlayback Component on Stage

8 In the **Behavior** panel, you will also find **Embedded Video Behaviors** that you can combine with **buttons** to create your own video controller.

9 Dragging the playhead allows you to preview the visuals, but in order to hear the audio you will need to select **Control > Test Movie**.

Rotoscoping

Or how to cheat at animation!

Rotoscoping is the process of drawing on film. It is named after the Rotoscope – a machine used by early animators such as Disney and the Fleischer Brothers to trace film of actors moving.

Embedded Video Behaviors

You can use the same technique in Flash. Video a scene or character and use this as reference for your animated drawings. Trace over by drawing on a layer above, adding keyframes on every one or two frames. Delete the video at the end and you will be left with accurate drawings of movement.

You can even Rotoscope your own Flashfiles:

1   To avoid a conventional motion tweened 'look', first create a motion tweened animation for speed and guidance.

2   Then on a new layer trace over each frame roughly, deliberately varying the placement of the line.

Before – Video in Flash

3   You will then get a style known in animation as '**boiling**' where the outlines seem to shimmer and shake.

Output Flash Animation at Full Broadcast Quality

Although Flash is increasingly being used to create low-budget animation

After – Rotoscoped Version

for television and commercials, it isn't actually designed to work with full size broadcast video. It specializes in video for the web. However, if you are aware of the technical issues involved, you can get around this and create Flash animation of **full broadcast quality**.

There may seem to be many complicated technical issues to consider when outputting from Flash for video, but if you want good quality results you must be aware of them right from the start.

You cannot use Flash to put animation directly onto video tape. To do this you will need to use a video-editing program like Adobe Premiere Pro, iMovie or Final Cut Pro. The animation must be exported from Flash with the correct settings to enable you to take it into a video-editing program and then export it onto tape.

Frame Rate and Frame Size

First of all, you must use a standard frame rate and size according to the system of video used in the part of the world in which you live.

Documents Settings for PAL/SECAM Video

This will be 25 frames per second if you are using the **PAL** video system. This is the type of video used in the UK, much of Europe, Africa and the Middle East, Australia, New Zealand, China and India.

The frame size for **PAL** is 768 × 576 (square) pixels.

Document Properties

Dimensions: | 640 px | (width)   x | 480 px | (height)

Match: (Printer) (Contents) (Default)

Background color: ☐▾

Frame rate: | 30 | fps

Ruler units: | Pixels | ⬍ |

(Make Default)   (Cancel) (OK)

Documents Settings for NTSC Video

If you live in the USA, Canada, South America, the Caribbean, Japan, Korea or Taiwan, however, you will be using the **NTSC** video system. This has a frame rate of 30 frames per second. (The figure is actually 29.97 but you can use a video-editing program to convert this for you.)

The frame size for **NTSC** is 640 × 480 (square) pixels.

There is also a third video system called **SECAM**, which also uses 25 frames per second and is used in France, Eastern Europe and some of Africa and the Middle East. It is similar to PAL, but uses a different color management system.

The frame size for **SECAM** is 768 × 576 (square) pixels.

Flash is not always able to play back 100% accurately from the Timeline with the full frame rate. If want to export your work to video and your timing is important to you, export test movies regularly and play them in your editing software.

Pixel Aspect Ratio

In Chapter 5 *Importing Images*, we looked at bitmap images and how they are made up of tiny little square pixels.

Digital video is a type of bitmap. However, it doesn't use square pixels, but rectangular or **non-square pixels**.

Flash cannot create files with non-square pixels – it works with square pixels.

So make your Flash movies with the square pixel frame sizes given above and use a video-editing program to convert them to non-square pixels for you.

If you do not use the square pixel frame sizes given above, your images may appear squashed or stretched when viewed on video.

Importing DV and Flash

As Flash is not specifically designed as a video-editing program, it does not actually import video with 100% accurately. This is because Flash works in **square** pixels and DV is in **non-square** pixels. As a result, imported video may be slightly **squashed** or **stretched**.

Here's what to do about it.

This PAL Video has Been Squashed on Import

Rescale Horizontally by 106.7%

This NTSC Video
has been Stretched
on Import

Rescale Horizontally by
88.9%

Frames vs. Fields

When you create animation in Flash, you can look at all of the individual frames that go into making it up.

Frame   Lower field   Raster lines   Upper field

Frames and Fields – Not to Scale!

Although video is commonly thought of in terms of frames, each **frame** of footage shot on video is actually divided into two **fields**.

These two **fields** are **interlaced** and when viewed one after the other, they form one whole frame. The interlaced lines are called **raster lines**. This is why the image stutters when you press pause on your video player. You are not looking at a complete image but at one half of it.

So although we think of **PAL** or **SECAM** video in terms of **25 frames per second** it is more accurate to say it is *50 fields per second*.

Similarly, although we think of **NTSC** video in terms of **30 frames per second** it is more accurate to say it is *60 fields per second*.

Flash cannot create animation in fields per second – only frames per second.

Using a video-editing program will convert animation created in Flash into fields per second for you.

Why bother about fields if your editing program will create them for you?

When you put your Flash animation on to video and the frames are converted into fields, **hairline** or **one pixel lines** and **thin, small fonts** may appear to **flicker**.

So if you want your Flash animation to end up on video, make your lines no smaller than two pixels and use bold, chunky fonts, preferably 18 points and above.

Broadcast Safe Colors

Not only does video have its own specific frame rate, frame size, pixel aspect ratio and field issues, but it also has its own **color gamut**! A **color gamut** is a

Luminance   Chrominance   Saturation
Color Components

range of colors that a medium can represent. You can create many more colors on a computer than a video tape can record.

There are three components of color on video:

- **luminance** – brightness or image intensity or tonal value;

- **chrominance** – or hue – actual color;

- **saturation** – color intensity for example full red vs. pink.

If one of these levels is too intense or **illegal**, then you will get a smearing in the image when it is played back from video that is also known as **video bleed**.

There is no way to check for video bleed in Flash. This needs to be done in a video-editing program like Adobe Premiere or Final Cut Pro or a compositing program like Adobe After Effects.

Scopes in Premiere Pro Help You to Analyze the Color Components of Your Video

The following tips will help you to avoid video bleed:

- Don't use very bright colors. De-saturate bright reds and blues by 20–30%.

- White text on black (and vice versa) can turn out badly – use pale cream or gray instead of white.

- Put test versions onto video regularly and check them out on a properly calibrated monitor.

- Use color correction filters in your editing software as a last resort.

Over Scan

There is one final issue to consider when creating Flash movies for output to video and that is **over scan**.

Television sets have a slight curvature at the very edge. There is no standardization! Different models have different amounts.

What does this have to do with Flash?

If you don't take this into consideration part of your image may be unexpectedly cropped off at the sides.

Safe Title and Action Zones

Keep in mind the **safe title** and **safe action** zones indicated in the diagram above.

Keep all of your important action within the **safe action** zone and all of your text titling within the **safe title** zone.

Now you know all about how to produce animation in Flash that will work well on video tape. Chapter 15 *Cross-media Publishing* covers the process of exporting from Flash to different delivery media.

CHAPTER 13
DESIGNING FOR CROSS-MEDIA

Our 21st Century world is full of information. In cities you can find information on every corner with interactive street kiosks, animated billboards, Internet cafes, TVs in homes and shop windows, people with arrays of small, portable devices such as Pocket PCs or PDAs, mobile phones and VCD players.

Our 21st Century World

You can create content for all of these different media and devices with Flash. Vector graphics programs, like Flash, are resolution independent and ideal to use for exporting to all different types of media. The same Flash file can be exported for a mobile phone movie or a poster campaign without loss of quality.

It is seductive to use exactly the same design across all of these different output devices, however each different device that you can create Flash content for has its own set of limitations. Each one has a different screen size and resolution, different bandwidth and frame rate. Some of them also use different color models.

In addition, a design composition that works well on a billboard poster may be impossible to see in any detail on a small PDA handset.

All of this needs to be considered when you are starting your project, because your output will influence your input. Be prepared to make subtle changes to your original design.

It is also important to consider exactly whom you want to communicate with. Define the goals of your project – who are you aiming it at and why would they be interested? Look at a range of examples of work from competitors and think about their pros and cons.

So, your first step in planning a Flash project is thinking – '*where* will I use this?' and '*who* do I want to see this?' In other words who is your **target audience** and what will be your **delivery medium**.

Planning a Web Site

Let us focus on designing web sites, because there is not enough space in a little Easy Guide to consider all the possible delivery media in depth. Many of these considerations can also be applied to other media.

As a starting point in the design and planning process, think about the following questions:

- What kind of computers do you think that the people who will look at your web site will have – lowest common denominator or latest high tech, Mac, PC, a mixture?

- Do you think they will have large monitors, small laptop screens or medium sized monitors?

- Do you think they will have the latest versions of a browser such as Internet Explorer or Netscape loaded on their machines as well as all the latest multimedia plug-ins?

- Do you think they'll be looking at your site at work with a fast broadband connection or at home with a slow domestic modem?

- Could they be 'looking' at your site with audio: using screen reading software?

- Could they be browsing from non-computers such as WAP phones, PDAs, interactive TV or Sega's Dreamcast?

All of these questions effect the overall dimensions of your project in pixels as well as the complexity and size of your files.

When you have made some decisions about your web site, you can start to plan your content. **What** are all the pieces of information that you want to include? **How** will they fit together? Draw a **flow chart** to help you. A **flow chart** is a good way to work out on paper the connections between the different pieces of information that you have.

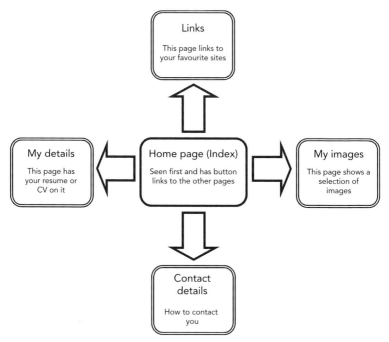

A Flow Chart Plan for an Portfolio

It is also very important to plan **where** to put all the different files that you create for your web site and how you will **name** them. As you are working keep a note of the following:

- Lists of different files or assets – **what are** all of the files that make up your web site including tests, research, scans and sources files?

- Naming conventions – what did you **name** them?

- Storage location for all documents belonging to your web site – **where** did you put them?

Information Architecture

When you are designing a web site, what you are doing is designing a way for the user to navigate through a mass of information. You should try to make this journey as straightforward as possible. When you have been working on a project for some time, it may seem obvious to you how to find your way around it. Other people who have not seen your project before may not find it so easy. The 'buzz' word right now is '**usability**'. How useable is your site? Try to test your site on friends and colleagues before you upload it to the web.

Try not to use the cliches of conventional web design – try new ideas. Be inspired by maps, journeys, roads, cities, buildings, stories – all of these involve moving from one piece of information to another.

Successful design is a mixture of coherent and logical structure and visual organization. Information should be structured so that it is clear and easily accessible. Use the following tips to make your site easy to navigate:

- try to be no more than two clicks away from either the home page or a site plan on any page;

- have clear links and back buttons on each page;

- build in several alternative routes to information;

- design for speed – use small files for a fast download time;

- maintain a visual identity with a consistency of color, design, icons and navigation throughout the site – people get used to a system;

- the form of your site should follow its function – superfluous graphics and animation can increase your download time without giving your user the information that they came to your site to find.

Finally, think of reasons why people might want to return to your site again in the future. This is also known as '**sticky content**'. Some examples of this could be:

- games;
- up to date information;
- entertaining animation;
- extensive links;
- competitions;
- web cam;
- chat rooms;
- send a greetings card;
- forum;
- message board.

Design for the Web

There are several approaches to using Flash for the web. The entire web site could be created in Flash and put on one single host HTML page, perhaps loading external files to save on file size. On the other hand, you could create a conventional HTML hyperlinked web site and add Flash elements to individual pages as required.

Size

There are two types of size to consider when designing for the web:

1   *Web page dimensions* – measured in pixels;

2   *File sizes* – measured in kilobytes.

The shape of the web page that you will be designing is in landscape format and important information should be at the top of page or '*above the fold*'.

People are used to accessing information quickly and may find it irritating to have to scroll to the right or downwards in order to see the whole site.

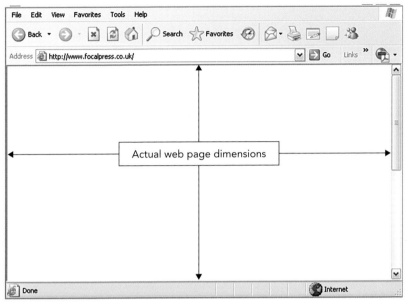

Address http://www.focalpress.co.uk/

Actual web page dimensions

The Browser Application

The browser program itself takes up space with menus, toolbars and scrollbars. Safe recommendations for web page sizes, which will fit the following monitor resolutions, are:

Screen Dimensions	Width	Height
640 × 480	600	300
800 × 600	760	420
1024 × 768	955	600

These dimensions do not take into consideration scroll bars, which will take up extra space.

The other aspect of size to consider is **file size**. Different web users have different bandwidths to contend with. Not all of your target audience may have access to a fast ISDN or broadband line.

Web access from mobile phones is common in Japan and South Korea, but not in the USA or most European countries where users prefer to surf from their computers.

A recent statistic states that 64% of people accessing the Internet from home are doing so with domestic modems and only 36% have broadband.

However, the situation is reversed with people surfing the web at work – 69% of them are using broadband with only 31% of work users having narrowband.

It is often said that sites, which take more than 20 seconds to load, will lose 50% of their visitors.

Web users do, indeed, have short attention spans. Statistics from **http://www.nielsen-netratings.com** show that the worldwide average duration of a web page viewed at home is 48 seconds and a few seconds more for viewing at work. This includes both **loading** and **reading** time.

An average domestic modem of **56 kbps** is measured in **kilobits** per second. If you take into consideration the fact that images are measured in *kilobytes* (a slightly different unit of measure) and that connection speeds are slower than expected because of the traffic of other users on the web, the actual speed of transmission translates to more like **4 kilobytes per second**.

So for a page to load in **20 seconds** it should be no **bigger than 80 kilobytes**, preferably **less**. This means your entire swf Flash file should be no more than 80 kilobytes. However, if you expect your audience to be mainly viewing your site from work, you could afford to make it slightly larger.

A typical **web banner** size is 468 × 60 pixels and around 15 kilobytes or less. The entire animated cycle should stay within a 3 seconds time limit and it should be possible to read all of the text within 2 seconds. Keep the frame rate between **10–15** frames per second. This is a good frame rate range to use in general for web animation.

Color

The use of color in web design is always going to be **approximate**. The display of color across different platforms and monitors can be unpredictable. Images can appear darker on a PC monitor and every user may have their monitor calibrated in a slightly different way.

Some people are using monitors that can display millions of colors while others can only display 256. Mac and PCs show two slightly different sets of 256 colors and only 216 overlap. These 216 colors are known as a **web safe palette** and are the only ones that can be guaranteed across both platforms.

Web safe Colors
in Color Swatch
Panel

Colors on the web are described using **hexadecimal code** – a combination of six letters and numbers for example white is #FFFFFF and black is #000000. Flash allows you to work with web safe colors. You can enter hexadecimal code directly in the **Color Mixer** panel or choose from the **Web 216** color palette in the **Color Swatches** panel options.

If you are designing for a corporate client who wants to maintain their brand identity through the use of certain colors or if you yourself want to restrict the number of colors that you use, you can create your own customized **color palette**. This is done in the **Color Swatches** panel:

1   To ensure that the colors you use are all web safe, load the **web safe palette** in the **Color Swatches** panel by choosing **Color Swatches Options > Web 216**.

Hexadecimal Code in the Color Mixer Panel

2 Then delete the colors that you **don't** want to use by selecting them and then **Delete Swatch** from the **Color Swatches Options** menu.

3 Select **Color Swatches Options** > **Clear Colors** to remove all of the colors in the **Color Swatches** panel apart from black and white.

4 Next mix up the colors that you **do** want to use in the **Color Mixer** panel and choose **Color Mixer Options** > **Add Swatch**. This will add the new colors to the **Color Swatches** panel.

5 To export your new color palette, select **Color Swatches** Options > Save Colors. Name your color palette and save it as a **CLR (Flash Color Set)** file.

6 You can now import this color palette into any Flash project by choosing **Color Swatches Options** > **Replace Colors**. This will replace the contents of the **Color Swatches** panel.

7 Alternatively, **Color Swatches Options** > **Add Colors** will add your custom color palette to the contents of the **Color Swatches** panel.

A Restricted Palette of
Corporate Colors in the
Color Swatches Panel

Typography

There are pros and cons to using the **HTML** of the host web page to display text
as opposed to creating all of the text in **Flash**.

Standard **HTML** text on a web page will load very fast, but the text formatting
possibilities available are not as extensive as that available in Flash. Also, positioning and formatting are imprecise.

Creating text in **Flash** gives you much more precision in positioning and formatting. However, the text contained within a Flash movie will not be seen until the
whole movie has loaded. It can also sometimes be more difficult to read than
HTML text.

Finally, with either method of creating text, unless you have turned the text into
a graphic, fonts can appear larger on a PC rather than a Mac. It is important to
test your designs on both platforms.

Usability

Flash has huge potential for the creation of fantastic animation and interactive
games, however if these are badly designed you can end up with a site that
alienates the user.

There is a lot of debate in the world of web design about the gratuitous use of Flash elements, which lack integration with the content and show the talents of the designer rather than enhancing the communication of ideas.

Avoid this! Make sure your intro movie has a **skip** button for users who have visited your site before. Keep your graphics and animation lean, mean and relevant. Looping movies can also be seen by some as annoying on the web – think before you loop!

Another issue that can arise with the usability of Flash web sites is **disability access**. A growing number of visually impaired web surfers are using audio browsers which 'speak' the contents of the screen or text only browsers. Legislation is being introduced in many countries around the world for the adoption of accessibility standards. For example, in the USA, Section 508 prohibits federal agencies from commissioning web sites, which are not accessible to people with disabilities.

The standards used are from the Worldwide Web Consortium and you can find more information about them and the whole issue of web content accessibility at **http://www.w3.org/WAI**.

Flash contains an **accessibility** panel, which allows you to add accessibility features to your site. This is discussed in the next chapter. Other general design tips for creating sites, which are easier for partially sighted or visually impaired viewers to use are:

- Use sans serif fonts – they can be clearer to read.
- Make sure there is a clear contrast between the background and text colors.
- Use a simple layout.
- Have a text only alternative for your site.

Planning for Animation

If you are creating an animation in Flash, it will save you time to plan it all out beforehand with a **storyboard**. This could be quite roughly done if it is just for your own use – a few scribbles on the back of an envelope. On the other hand, you may spend some time getting your storyboard to look good if you want to sell your idea to someone else. Spending time on the planning stage will save you time in the long run.

If you are intending to create an interactive story or game with several possible plot twists, then you could plan this out with a combination of a flow chart and a storyboard. Pinning index cards or sticky 'post-it' notes onto a wall, so that you can re-arrange them, can be a useful process.

It is also good practice to plan your characters. Consider how they will look from different angles and with different expressions. Sketch these all out on one sheet. This is called a **model** sheet in traditional animation.

The storyboard is useful for planning a sequence of events and can be used to create an **animatic**, which allows you to test out the timing of your animation. Here's how:

An Example of a Quick Storyboard

1   Scan all of your storyboard drawings in low resolution – to keep the file sizes down.

2   Check that your frame rate and document sizes are correct for your delivery medium – web, video, etc.

3   Put each drawing on a separate keyframe and give it extra frames to last for the time that you think that sequence should take.

4   Preview to see if your timing works and your story makes sense. Show to friends and colleagues and ask their opinion.

CHAPTER 14
PUTTING FLASH ON THE WEB

Now that you have designed and produced a slick, all-singing, all-dancing
Flash web site, what are the practicalities of organizing your site, adding the
finishing touches and putting it on the web?

Project Management Tips

It doesn't take long for a seemingly simple project to become very complicated.
You can end up with many different assets, objects and layers. The following tips
will help you to organize your project efficiently:

1   Always name your layers after what is on them.

**In this Animation of a Character Walking, Each Layer is Named After the Body Part
on it. Labels Have Been Added to Blank keyframes on a Layer in the Timeline to
Mark Key Stages in the Walk Cycle**

2   Create a '**Labels**' layer and add comments to remind you of key stages in
your animation.

3   If you are using lots of layers, simplify your Timeline by using layer
folders.

4   If you forgotten which layer an object is on, turn the visibility on and off –
by clicking on the **eye icon** on the layer – for all of your layers until you
find the correct one.

5   Keep your Library tidy and keep your assets in obviously named
folders.

6 If you have more than one Flash project open you can add a Library item from one project into the other. Flash will add it to the Library of your current file.

7 At the end of your project, choose **Library** > **Options** > **Select Unused Items** and then delete the items that you haven't used.

Drop down menu allows you to select the library of whichever files you have open

The Use Count column in the Library

The Use Count Column in the Library

8 **Library** > **Options** > **Keep Use Count Update** shows how many times you've used each item if you scroll through the columns at the right.

9 When working on a complex project use **Movie Explorer**. **Window** > **Other Panels** > **Movie Explorer** shows all the elements in your current scene. The buttons along the top enable you to filter which kind of object you want to see.

10 **CTRL/RIGHT-CLICK** on any of the elements and choose **Go to Location** to find it.

To show ActionScripts
To show buttons, movie clips and graphics | To show video, sounds and bitmaps
To show frames and layers
To show text | To customize which items to show

The Movie Explorer Window

The History Panel

The **History** panel allows you to see a list of the steps you have taken in your project. It can be accessed by selecting: **Window > Other Panels > History**.

This panel shows a list of the steps you took when working on your Flash project. You can go back in the list and delete stages if you want, but you cannot re-order them. Choose **File > Save and Compact** to remove deleted stages from your document.

The History Panel

By default, there are 100 steps recorded in the History panel. This can be customized in the **Preferences** where you can change it to any number between 2 and 9999.

Tips for Lowering File Sizes

When creating web sites with Flash, it is important to try to keep your file size as small as possible – not everyone has broadband. Here are some tips to help you keep your file size down:

1 Animating with **symbols** rather than using frame-to-frame animation will keep the file size down. This is because after you have defined your symbol you are making alterations to them on each keyframe rather than starting a whole new piece of information like you do in frame-by-frame animation. Consequently on each keyframe you are only recording the changes that have been made to the original symbol. This takes up less computer processing power than with frame-by-frame animation which has new content on each keyframe.

2 Why not set yourself a challenge and try to design a character using only several copies of one symbol?

3 Animated bitmaps are huge! Use them sparingly.

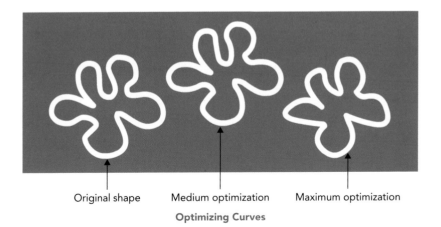

Original shape   Medium optimization   Maximum optimization

Optimizing Curves

Flash 8 ☒	Flash 8 ☒
⚠ The original shapes had 54 curves. The optimized shape has 38 curves. This is a 29% reduction.	⚠ The original shapes had 54 curves. The optimized shape has 20 curves. This is a 62% reduction.
[OK]	[OK]

Medium Optimization	Maximum Optimization

4 Another tip to reduce your file size is to **optimize** all your curves – in other words smooth them out and reduce their complexity. You can do this by selecting a curved shape and **Modify > Shape > Optimize**. You can modify fills as well as strokes.

5 **Softening Fill Edges** takes processor power and the edge has an annoying habit of getting left behind if you move the shape before grouping it with the edge. It is easier on file size to create a radial gradient fill, whose outer edge is the same as the background color of your documents – use the eyedropper to select the background color.

6 However, the use of gradients can also increase your file size and even the playback speed so keep them to a minimum.

7 Textured lines create a bigger file size so use solid lines where possible.

8 Reduce the number of fonts used, as fonts are embedded and result in a larger file size. Instead **break apart** text or use Flash **device** fonts. Using these generic **_sans**, **_serif** or **_typewriter** fonts will reduce the overall file size because no additional font info will be saved in the file. This means that the user's default fonts are used – usually Arial, Times New Roman and Courier.

9 The more separate items you have animating at the same time, the more of a strain you'll put on the user's computer – not a problem if you plan to export your work for putting onto video – but not good for the web, so try to plan around this.

10 Use MP3 sound compression – it is the most efficient.

Testing Your Work

Control > Test Movie or **⌘/CTRL + RETURN/ENTER** opens a new window in which you can see a test version of your document at 100% magnification. This will give you a clear idea of what your final version will look like. The test version will loop by default and a temporary SWF version of the document will be exported with a filename based on the filename you have given your document as a **FLA** file.

In this testing environment there are different functions available in the menus.

Click on this ruler to view one frame in isolation

The red line indicates the level of real time download at your target modem speed

The Bandwidth Profiler

View > Bandwidth Profiler shows a frame-by-frame graph of the download sizes of each frame.

View > Simulate Download gives you a preview of how long your site will take to load.

View > Download Settings allows you to change the modem speed that you are simulating.

To exit the testing environment, click on the X of your test version to close it – as you would to close any other file.

Anatomy of a Web Site

How is a Web Site Put Together and Where Does Flash Fit in?

A web site consists of one or more hyperlinked **HTML** pages located on a host computer known as a **server**. It is accessed through the use of a **browser** program like Netscape or Internet Explorer.

In order to put a Flash document on the web, it needs to be exported in the **SWF** file format and put on an **HTML** page.

HTML is a very basic language, which is not able to do much more than **display** text and page formatting and **link** to other pages and what is sometimes known as '**rich content**' – in other words things like sound, video, images, Flash movies or games. Flash movies are used to create more complex content than HTML is able to produce on its own.

A Flash Document is Exported as an SWF File and Placed Within an HTML File in Order to be Shown on the WWW

Even though it is possible to create a whole site in Flash, you still need a web page to put this on. The first HTML page that your user comes to is always called **index.htm or .html**. This convention allows the browser program to automatically recognize that this is the first page of your site.

Don't worry, you won't have to write complex coding to get your Flash project on the web – web design programs like Dreamweaver or Go Live will do all the hard work for you. You can also get Flash itself to generate a web page that contains your Flash movie. This is done through **publishing** your document.

Exporting and Publish Settings

There are several different file formats to which you can export your Flash document. To view the most common options **File > Publish Settings** and then click on the **Formats** tab.

Click here to open a tab for your chosen format   Enter a filename here   Click here to set the file location

| Publish Settings | | |

Current profile: [Default]

| Formats | Flash | HTML | GIF | JPEG | PNG | QuickTime |

Type:
- ☑ Flash (.swf)
- ☑ HTML (.html)
- ☑ GIF Image (.gif)
- ☑ JPEG Image (.jpg)
- ☑ PNG Image (.png)
- ☐ Windows Projector (.exe)
- ☐ Macintosh Projector
- ☑ QuickTime (.mov)

File:
- yoursite.swf
- yoursite.html
- yoursite.gif
- yoursite.jpg
- yoursite.png
- yoursite.exe
- yoursite Projector
- yoursite.mov

The Publish Settings

Clicking on the **Flash** tab allows you to make choices about the **SWF** file that you will export.

Which version of Flash Player do you think your target users will have? Do you want to protect this file from anyone else being able to import it? Which order do you want your layers to load in?

Be sure to select **Compress Movie** for an optimum file size and enter a **JPEG quality**, which

Options: ☑ **Generate size report**

Generate Size Report

will be applied to any bitmaps you have used regardless of their original file format.

Generate size report exports a text file with details about the effect that different elements have on the overall file size.

Select the **HTML** tab to customize an HTML page, which will be used to display your Flash document.

Flash Version Detection

What will happen to your beautiful work in Flash if the web user looking at your web page doesn't have Flash player installed on their computer?

☑ **Detect Flash Version**   (**Settings...**)

↑

Click here to open the settings

Detect Flash Version

If you use Flash to generate a web page for you, selecting **Detect Flash Version** will allow you to divert users who do not have the correct version of Flash installed. Here's how:

index.html

This first page detects whether the user has Flash player installed

YES

page1.html

Go to full Flash web site

NO

alternativepage1.html

Go to alternative page

Flow Chart

1 If the correct version of Flash Player is detected, your user will be automatically taken to your Flash movie. If they do not, they will be diverted to an alternative page.

2 Click on the word **Settings** to open the Version Detection Settings.

3 Enter a name for the page that will do the version detection. When you publish this document, Flash will generate a movie called **flash_detection.swf**, which will go on the first page (**index.html** in the example above).

Version Detection Settings

Requirements
Flash Version: Major Revision: Minor Revision:
6   0   0

Filenames
Detection File (first target file):
index.html

Content File:
page1.html

Alternate File:
alternativepage1.html

◉ Generate Default
○ Use Existing (select filename)   Browse...

Use Defaults   Cancel   OK

Version Detection Settings

4 Enter a name for the **Content File**. This is the page with the Flash movie on (**page 1.html** in the example above).

5 You have two choices as to where to go if the user doesn't have the correct version of Flash player:

- **Generate Default** will create a page similar to the one in the diagram below.

- **Use Existing** allows you to choose a page that you have created already. This is a good choice if you want to make a site that is truly accessibility friendly. The **alternative** page (**alternativepage1.html** in the example above) could take the user to a simple text-only HTML version of your site, which is either free from any text formatting or uses style sheets to format the text while keeping the code clean.

You don't have the latest version of Macromedia Flash Player.

This web site makes use of Macromedia®Flash™software. You have an old version of Macromedia Flash Player that cannot play the content we've created.

GET macromedia
FLASH
PLAYER
Why not download and install the latest version now? It will only take a moment.

Macromedia and Flash are trademarks of Macromedia, Inc.

Alternative Page Generated By Flash

Movie Dimensions

Another important decision you have to make is the size of your web site. In the previous chapter, the issue of different monitor sizes was referred to. If your site has been created in order to be seen on the smallest monitor resolutions – 600 × 300 pixels – it will seem very small on a larger monitor. There is a way to get round this. Here's how:

1 It is possible to make your HTML page – and the Flash file it contains – **scalable**. In other words, it will change size according to the size of the monitor that the user has.

2 If you take advantage of this scalable option, be careful with bitmap images as then may become pixelated when enlarged by scaling.

HTML Publish Settings > Dimensions

3 If you choose **Match Movie** or **Pixels** as the **dimensions**, then the file will have a **fixed** or **absolute** size.

4 However, if you choose **Percent** it will have a **relative** size. In other words, the size will be a percentage of the space in the browser window and not fixed in an absolute pixel size.

Window Mode:	··· ·
	Default (Show all)
HTML alignment:	No border
	Exact fit
Scale:	✓ No scale

HTML Publish Settings > Scale

5 The scalability will be effected by the option you have chosen in the **Scale** options:

- **Default (Show all)** – scaled in proportion, if window is scaled out of proportion bars will appear at the side.

- **No border** – scaled in proportion, if window is scaled out of proportion the file will be cropped.

- **Exact fit** – if window is scaled out of proportion the file will be stretched or squashed to fit.

- **No scale** – file is not rescaled.

When you have chosen all options required for your Flash and HTML pages, click on the **Publish** button to export an HTML page and an SWF file.

The HTML page or pages can be opened in any web design program and edited.

Uploading

Having now gone through the process of creating and exporting a Flash web site – **how does it get on the Internet?**

Your first step is to buy some **space** on a web server **and** a domain **name**. Buying a domain name on its own does not automatically get you web space. A search on the Internet will lead you to many companies offering free web space and names. When you read the small print, though, you usually have to accept their advertizing on your site – you don't get something for nothing.

When you buy a space and a name you will be given a password and details of where on the web to upload your files to – make a note of all this information and keep it safe.

The uploading process is usually done through **ftp** or file transfer protocol. This is just a way of sending files from your computer to a server computer somewhere else in the world.

Web design programs like Dreamweaver or GoLive or simple ftp programs like Fetch can be used for this.

As mentioned earlier in this chapter, a **Flash** document is **displayed** by an **HTML** page.

The **SWF** file that you export from Flash is **linked** to the **HTML** page and not **embedded** within it.

So when you transfer all of the files to the server computer, you need to include both the **HTML – container** – file and the **SWF – contents** – file.

Flash on the WWW

Now you know how to export your Flash project and put it on the WWW, let's look at some issues that are relevant to Flash web sites.

Creating Pre-loaders

Even if you have heeded my advice in Chapter 13 and created a very small, mean and lean Flash file for your web site, it may take a few seconds for a web user to load your page. For this reason, it is a good idea to use a **pre-loader**.

A **pre-loader** is a small starter movie that plays while the main site is loading. It should keep your users attention. Pre-loaders can be very complex to create and require a good understanding of ActionScripting.

Here's how to cheat and create a simplified version of your own using **components**. **Components** are pre-created **movie clip symbols** with scripting attached. They can make life easier for you.

1   You should have already completed your whole web site and exported it (for the sake of this example) as **your_whole_site.swf**. As this example is a cheat, it relies on your web site having a solid background – in other

words put a rectangle of color in the background. Don't just use the background color of your document as usual.

2 Make a new Flash document. Make sure that it has exactly the same pixel dimensions and background color as in the previous one.

3 Now make a **movie clip** symbol with a very small piece of looped animation in it. This is what your user will see while waiting. Put it on a layer called *animation*.

4 Make another layer called *loader* and make sure this layer is active.

5 Choose **Window** > **Components** to open the **Components** panel.

An Animated Loop in a Movie Clip
Symbol on a Layer Called Animation

6 Expand the **UI** (User Interface) **Components** and click and drag a **Loader** component onto the Stage.

7 In the **Properties Inspector**, give the loader an instance name like *cmpLoad*.

8 Make sure the **Loader** component has the **same** dimensions as your **original** Flash movie web site by entering its pixel dimensions into the **W** and **H** options in the Properties Inspector.

UI Components

Loader Parameters

9   Then use the **Align** panel to **align horizontal** and **vertical center** with **To Stage** selected – makes sure this is perfectly aligned.

10   Make sure the **Parameters** tab is checked in the Properties Inspector.

11   Leave **autoLoad** and **scaleContent** to true. This means that your original site will automatically load into the *cmpLoad* Loader component and will be sized to fit its new container.

12   In **contentPath** enter the name of the original SWF file: your_main_site.swf. This file must be in the same folder as the current document for this to work.

13   Make sure the *loader* layer is above the *animation* layer.

14   Press ⌘/**CTRL + RETURN/ENTER** to test.

15   What has happened is that you have created a very small SWF movie that plays an animated loop. As this loop is within a movie clip symbol it will keep repeating independently of the Timeline.

16   While it is doing this it is also loading your whole site through the use of a Loader component.

17   When your whole site has loaded into the component it will hide the animated loop because the loop is on the layer above.

Accessibility

One of the important things to think about when designing a web site is accessibility to your site for visually impaired users. One option you have available to you is to create a plain text only HTML version of your site. It is also possible to add accessibility features within a Flash movie through the use of the

Accessibility panel. This makes it straightforward to add accessibility features to your Flash projects that will make them easier to use with audio browsers.

Remember that lots of countries have passed laws on disability and discrimination. In many cases, accessibility is a legal requirement and the responsibility for this lies with the designer/developer. That means you!

1 To open this panel, go to **Window > Other Panels > Accessibility**.

2 When the background of the Stage is clicked on and the **Document** properties are showing in the Properties Inspector, you will see the following settings in the **Accessibility** panel:

3 **Make Movie Accessible** is on by default. This allows accessibility information about your whole movie to be passed to a screen reader program by Flash Player. It will allow the software to 'read' out loud the names and descriptions you have given.

The Accessibility Panel

4 Add a **name** and a **description**, which summarizes all the elements on screen that do not contain text. It will help users who are browsing with a screen reader if you include information about the layout and navigation controls.

5 **Flash Player** automatically provides a name for **static text** and **dynamic text**, which is actually the same as the contents of the text, so text does not need to be labeled through the **Accessibility** panel.

6 **Make Child Objects Accessible** is used for information nested inside **Movie clips**.

7 **Auto label** is used to automatically label objects on the stage with the text associated with them. The objects that this applies to are **buttons**, **movie clips** and any Flash **SWF** files that you may have imported.

8 In order for this to work, you must first make sure that you have given them instance names in the **Properties Inspector**. Names for **buttons**

will be based on any text you have used in your button. **Movie clip** symbols or **SWF** Flash files will be based on their instance name.

9   Deselect this option if you would prefer to add your own information to individual items.

Adding Accessibility Information to a Button

10   To add your own information, click on each **button, movie clip** or **SWF** file that you might have on your page and add the relevant information in the **Accessibility** panel.

11   Animation can confuse screen reader software as the content is changing, so select any animation and deselect the **Make Object Accessible** option.

12   For more information on this issue, go to the Macromedia web site: **http://www.macromedia.com/software/Flash/productinfo/accessibility.**

SWF File Metadata

Internet search engines, such as Google, use metadata to search for information. This is data **about** your file that you can add to. In the past, HTML files could contain metadata, but Flash files couldn't. However, as of Flash 8, you can add metadata to Flash documents improving their searchability on the Web. Here's how:

1 Select **Modify** > **Document**.

Document Properties

T̲itle:	name of your project
D̲escription:	add metadata here, i.e. key words and phrases that you would like WWW Search Engines to associate with this page

Adding Metadata in the Document Properties Window

2 Add a descriptive **title** that contains searchable terms.

3 Add a **description**, which could contain searchable keywords, author and copyright information, and short descriptions about the content and its purpose.

4 You will need to specify a **title** and **description** for each Flash document that you create. They are the only things that can't be stored when you create your own **default** document settings.

CHAPTER 15
CROSS-MEDIA PUBLISHING

It is not possible in one little Easy Guide to cover all of the different media that you could export to from Flash. This chapter covers export from Flash to print, video, DVD and stand-alone projectors.

In the previous chapter we looked at using the **publish settings** to export SWF and HTML files to create output for the Web. It is possible to customize these settings to create different kinds of output for different kinds of media.

Publishing Profiles

Publishing profiles are a way of saving information about your export options that you can go back to and reuse. When you export for many possible cross-media outputs, you can save a profile in the **Publish Settings** window for each output type.

The Publish Settings

To create a profile:

1   Select **File > Publish Settings** and then click on the **add a profile** button. Give the new profile a name.

Create New Profile

2   Then select the formats required and the necessary options for your
new profile.

Profile Choices

3   You will now be able to select it from the different profiles you have
created.

4   If you want to reuse this profile in another document or even share it
with a colleague so that can use the same settings, click on the **export
profile** button and select **export**. This creates an **XML** file, which can
be used in other Flash document.

Exporting Stills

If you want to export individual still images, for example to use as a
printed graphic, go to the frame you want to export and then select
File > Export > Export Image.

If you want to export for print, choose **Adobe Illustrator** as the file type. This
will maintain all the vector parts of your image.

It is always good practice to check with your printer exactly which file formats
they will accept and what resolution they work at.

Remember to create an extra margin of image, as your printer will need an
excess 35 millimeter bleed off the edge for cropping purposes.

Images in Flash are in RGB color, so convert this file to CMYK in an imaging
software, like Freehand, Illustrator or Photoshop. This is the type of color space

used for the print process. You can also add crop marks, if needed, in an imaging software.

Vector graphics are resolution independent. If your printer needs to print from a bitmap format, make sure that you export with a resolution of at least 300 dots per inch.

Exporting with Audio

In the **Flash Publish Settings**, you can set the quality of audio that you want for streaming or event sounds in an **SWF**.

The audio compression is set to MP3 by default. This is a very effective type of compression and under normal circumstances you can accept the default settings here.

Audio stream: MP3, 16 kbps, Mono	(Set)
Audio event: MP3, 16 kbps, Mono	(Set)
☐ Override sound settings	

Click on the Set Button to Open the Audio Settings

Sound Settings

(OK)

Compression: [MP3 ▲▼]   (Cancel)

Preprocessing: ☑ Convert stereo to mono

Bit rate: [16 kbps ▲▼]

Quality: [Fast ▲▼]

Sound Export Settings

These defaults will be applied to all of the sounds in your SWF file regardless of the format you imported them in as. So even if you imported them as a **WAV** file, they can still be exported as MP3.

Selecting **Override sound settings** will enable you to attach individual types of audio settings to individual audio files within your Flash movie.

Individual settings can be attached to sound files in the Library. Select the file you want to add individual settings to, choose **Library** > **Options** > **Properties** and choose the settings you want to use from the **Compression** options.

Exporting for Video Output

Exporting for video is a matter of **File** > **Export** > **Export Movie** and choosing your required file format. The most common choices are **QuickTime Video, AVI, JPEG sequence or Adobe Illustrator sequence**.

The advantage of exporting as a movie file like QuickTime or AVI is that you only have one file to think about and it will also contain any sounds that you might have added. Exporting as a sequence of numbered still images will sometimes give the best quality. Experiment until you find the file format that works best for your particular project.

In Chapter 12 **Video**, we examined how to create animation with the correct frame rate and size, square pixels, broadcast safe color levels and all within safe title and action zones.

As we have previously discussed, Flash creates vector graphics. When you export a moving image file format, the vector Flash frames are converted into bitmap video frames. The only problem here is that after this conversion process, sometimes your lines can look '**jagged**'.

The following tips should help you to avoid this:

1 Try to avoid emphatic straight lines at an **angle**.

2 The problem seems to be amplified with strong **color contrasts** between the angled line and the background, so **avoid** this where possible.

3 In your video-editing software use a **motion** or **gaussian blur** of around 0.7 to eliminate this.

4 If you have a copy of Adobe After Effects, export from Flash as an **Adobe Illustrator sequence**. This is my personal preferred option, because this method seems to produce files at optimum quality. After

Effects will recognize the sequence of numbered files as a movie and will maintain the vector quality. SWF files can also be imported into After Effects if QuickTime 5 or above is installed on your machine.

5 If you are using Final Cut Pro, export from Flash as a **Version 4 SWF**. Final Cut Pro can import an SWF if it is in version 4 or earlier.

About Compression

Digital video files can be very large. When you export from your Flash **FLA** file into a **QuickTime** or **AVI** movie, you can use compression to keep the file size down. Compression is basically a mathematical formula that is used to squeeze the maximum amount of information into the minimum storage space.

After you have chosen **File > Export > Export Movie** and **QuickTime** or **AVI** as your file type, then select **smooth** and to **compress video** select a type of **compression** or **CODEC** from the list available.

There will be different choices of compression available depending on whether you have chosen **QuickTime** or **AVI** and also depending on which CODECs are installed on your particular computer.

If you want to put your Flash animation onto video, choose **DV PAL** or **NONE** or the **CODEC that came with your capture card.** It is best practice to take your animation out of Flash at the highest possible quality and then to add compression at the final stage in your editing program.

Make sure the quality is at the **highest setting**. Experiment to see which compression type gives the best quality for your particular project.

Compositing Your Flash Movie

Compositing is the process of combining computer-generated animation with video. This can be done by importing video into Flash and creating animation on layers above the video clip.

However, you may wish to do this in an editing or post-production program, which has many more tools for working with video.

In order to seamlessly combine animation with video, it is best to create a sequence of animation with a transparent background.

The easiest way to do this is to export an Adobe Illustrator sequence to After Effects. All areas of the original in which the background color of the document were showing will be automatically transparent in After Effects.

Flash Animation Combined with Video in After Effects

In order to make sure that your Illustrator sequence is interpreted at the highest quality in After Effects, while in After Effects select the file in the **Project** window and then **File > Interpret footage > Main > More options > Antialiasing > More accurate**. Also, in After Effects, make sure that **continuously rasterize** is enabled for the layer.

You get the same effect of a transparent background if you export a PNG sequence from Flash and take it into After Effects. However, PNG files are bitmaps and will not retain the vector scalability like the Illustrator file format.

Alpha Channels

How Did That Work?

The areas that are transparent were recorded in an **alpha channel**. This is a channel of information contained in the file about transparency. Only certain file formats and certain types of compression can contain alpha channels.

If you want to create transparency in a QuickTime or AVI file, it is a slightly more complex process:

1   Go into the **Color Mixer** and make a color with 0% Alpha.

2 From the **Color Mixer options** choose **Add Swatch** and the transparent color will be added to the **Color Swatches** panel.

Transparent Color Swatch
(Circled)

3 This transparent color can now be chosen as the background color for the document in the Properties Inspector or by choosing **Modify > Document**.

Export QuickTime Video		

	Width	Height	
Dimensions:	768	X 576	pixels
	☑ Maintain aspect ratio		
Format:	32 bit color (alpha cha... ↕		
	☑ Smooth		
Compressor:	Animation ↕		
Quality:	▬▬▬▬▬▬▬▬▬▽		

OK

Cancel

Exporting a QuickTime with an Alpha Channel

4 On a Mac, export as a **QuickTime Video** with **Animation** compression and **32-bit color (alpha channel)**. The PC equivalent is to export as a **Windows AVI** with a type of compression that can support alpha channels and is loaded on your system – like **Intel Indeo Video** compression – and **32-bit color (alpha channel)**.

5 This file can now be taken into a video-editing program and alpha channel transparency can be utilized.

Putting Your Flash Movie onto Video

As previously discussed, follow these stages to put Flash animation onto **video**:

1 Create animation in a Flash document with the correct frame rate and square pixels frame size for the region in which you live – NTSC, PAL or SECAM.

2   **File** > **Export** > **Export Movie** and chose a file format compatible with your video-editing program.

3   Take this movie into your video editing program.

4   Use the video editing program to record the animation onto tape.

Putting Your Flash Movie onto DVD

Putting Flash animation onto **DVD** is a slightly different process.

A DVD consists of **MPEG** video files, **menu** and **navigation** information woven together into a specific data structure. All of these files must be created and stored with the correct conventions in order to be read on a DVD player.

You can't create files directly out of Flash that will play on a DVD player straight away.

If you are working on a **Mac** export **QuickTime** movies from Flash. Bring these into a DVD authoring software like DVD Studio Pro or iDVD. These will create MPEGs and DVD menu structures for you.

If you are working on **Windows**, Adobe Premiere will accept AVI or QuickTime movies. You can use it to create MPEGs and author basic DVDs. You can also bring QuickTimes, AVIs or MPEGs into Adobe Encore to create DVDs with more complex menu structures.

Exporting Projectors

Projectors are stand-alone applications that do not require the user to have Flash Player installed on their machine. They are useful for authoring CD-ROMs and emailing. You will need to create one version for Mac and one version for Windows users.

Be aware that projectors are bigger in file size than SWFs.
Choose **File** > **Publish Settings** and select **Windows Projector (.exe)** and **Macintosh Projector** in the **Format** options. There are no options to customize in the **Publish Settings** for projectors.

If you want to create a CD-ROM that will automatically open on a PC, here's how:

1 **Publish** a **projector** file from Flash, for the sake of example let's call it ***myprojector.exe***.

2 Open up a text program like Notepad and type in:

[autorun]

open = myprojector.exe

3 This will automatically open your projector file when the CD is inserted.

4 Save this text file as an 'All Files (*.*)' and name it ***autorun.inf***.

5 Burn your CD-ROM with the ***autorun.inf***, and projector file in the root directory of the CD.

6 Unfortunately, this will only work on a PC and not on a Mac.

Creating a Hybrid CD

If you want to create a CD that will play on both Macs and PCs, first export both a Mac and PC projector. Then make sure that your CD burner can burn it as a **hybrid** CD, which will open on both platforms.

All of these links were correct at the time of going to press.

Web Usage Statistics

Nielsen/Net rating: http://www.nielsen-netratings.com

The Counter.com: http://www.counter.com

Macromedia: http://www.macromedia.com/software/player_census/flashplayer/

Web Design Info

Jakob Nielsen, the usability guru: http://www.useit.com

Web Monkey: http://hotwired.lycos.com/webmonkey

Accessibility

Worldwide Web Consortium: http://www.w3.org/WAI

Macromedia: http://www.macromedia.com/macromedia/accessibility/

More About Mobile Devices

Macromedia Mobile Devices site: http://www.macromedia.com/devnet/devices

Sound Resources on the Web

Free sound FX: http://www.flashkit.com/soundfx/

Free loops and FX: http://www.samplenet.co.uk

The Camarillos: http://www.thecamarillos.co.uk

Open source audio: http://www.archive.org follow links to > **audio** > **open source audio**

ActionScripting Tutorials on the Web

Flash Kit: http://www.flashkit.com/tutorials/Actionscripting/

Actionscript.org: http://www.actionscript.org/

Flash Guru: http://www.flashguru.co.uk/category/flash-tutorials/

Kirupa.com: http://www.kirupa.com/developer/actionscript/index.htm

Flash Animation Tutorials on the Web

Macromedia: http://www.macromedia.com/support/flash/design_animation.html

Flash Film Maker: http://www.flashfilmmaker.com/

Flash Kit: http://www.flashkit.com/tutorials/Animation/

Animation Resources on the Web

Animation World Network: http://www.awn.com

About animation: http://animation.about.com/

Further Reading on Character Animation

Blair, Preston. (1994). **Cartoon Animation**, Walter Foster Publishing.

Whitaker, Harold and Halas, John. (2002). **Timing for Animators**, Focal Press.

Williams, Richard. (2001). **The Animators Survival Guide**, Faber and Faber.

Further Reading on Motion Graphics

Curran, Steve. (2001). **Motion Graphics**, Rockport Publishers, Inc.

Goux, Melanie and Houff, James A. (2003). **> On Screen > In Time**, Rotovision.

Hall, Peter and Codrington, Andrea. (2000). **Pause: 59 Minutes of Motion Graphics**, Universe Publishing.

Woolman, Matt and Bellantoni, Jeff. (2000). **Moving Type**, Rotovision.

Further Reading on Flash

Michael, Alex. (2006). **Animating with Macromedia Flash 8**, Focal Press.

Michael, Alex and Rapo, Andrew. (2006). **Understanding Macromedia Flash8 ActionScript 2.0**, Focal Press.

Index

Focal Press www.focalpress.com

Join Focal Press online

As a member you will enjoy the following benefits:

- browse our full list of books available
- view sample chapters
- order securely online

Focal eNews

Register for eNews, the regular email service from Focal Press, to receive:

- advance news of our latest publications
- exclusive articles written by our authors
- related event information
- free sample chapters
- information about special offers

Go to www.focalpress.com to register and the eNews bulletin will soon be arriving on your desktop!

If you require any further information about the eNews or www.focalpress.com please contact:

USA
Tricia La Fauci
Email: t.lafauci@elsevier.com
Tel: +1 781 313 4739

Europe and rest of world
Lucy Lomas-Walker
Email: l.lomas@elsevier.com
Tel: +44 (0) 1865 314438

Catalogue

For information on all Focal Press titles, our full catalogue is available online at www.focalpress.com, alternatively you can contact us for a free printed version:

USA
Email: c.degon@elsevier.com
Tel: +1 781 313 4721

Europe and rest of world
Email: L.Kings@elsevier.com
Tel: +44 (0) 1865 314426

Potential authors

If you have an idea for a book, please get in touch:

USA
editors@focalpress.com

Europe and rest of world
ge.kennedy@elsevier.com